HIGHEST CALLING

Serving in the Royal Priesthood

LARRY LEA

Creation House
Lake Mary, Florida

Copyright © 1991 by Larry Lea
All rights reserved
Printed in the United States of America
Library of Congress Catalog Card Number: 91-70019
International Standard Book Number: 0-88419-289-X

Creation House
Strang Communications Company
600 Rinehart Road
Lake Mary, FL 32746
(407) 333-0600

This book or parts thereof may not be reproduced in any form without prior written permission of the publisher.

Unless otherwise noted, all Scripture quotations are from the New King James Version of the Bible. Copyright © 1979, 1980, 1982 by Thomas Nelson Inc., publishers. Used by permission.

Scripture quotations marked Amplified are from the Amplified Bible. Old Testament copyright © 1965, 1987 by the Zondervan Corporation. The Amplified New Testament copyright © 1954, 1958, 1987 by the Lockman Foundation. Used by permission.

Scripture quotations marked KJV are from the King James Version of the Bible.

CONTENTS

FOREWORD

I will never forget the feeling that came over me the day I received that telephone call from Larry Lea. I had met him only a few weeks earlier. He had come to Kilgore, Texas, to visit his parents. Since I had scheduled him to speak at a special youth rally at my church, he had stopped by to get better acquainted.

As we talked in my study at the First Assembly of God Church, Larry's pastor and friend, Howard Conatser, was in a Dallas hospital at the point of death.

The Lord seemed to give me the words Larry needed to hear. We talked and prayed for hours. I shared with him many of the things God had taught me about faith and prayer, and this young man seemed to soak them up like a dry sponge.

Not long afterward Howard Conatser went to be with the Lord. Understanding the principles of spiritual authority, Larry began to seek God about whom he was to look to as his pastor.

It was July 1978. Larry Lea's voice was clear on the phone: "Pastor Willhite, as I was shaving this morning God spoke to me and said *you* are my pastor. I am to put my ministry under your authority."

I was stunned. I remember thinking that the greater was bowing to the lesser. At the time Larry was not well-known, but he was certainly better known than I. Before I ever heard him speak, I knew that God had great plans for Larry Lea; that he, in fact, would have a ministry which would far exceed mine. I remember telling him not long afterward that he had the potential to influence the world as Billy Graham had.

There is no doubt that God has anointed this man to call the nation and the world to meaningful prayer. His books are now being translated into several languages and have had the same effect everywhere.

Paul makes it very clear in the first chapter of 1 Corinthians that God chooses the weak things to confound the strong and the foolish things to confound the wise. He chooses the base things and the things which are insignificant in the eyes of men to do His work. This is true of Larry and me. God did not look for the wisest, the strongest or the purest. Why? So that men will give God the glory for what He does through earthen vessels.

Highest Calling is a book which will encourage the reader to rise to his calling to be a priest and, in that priestly office, to intercede to God on behalf of others. Many, indeed, are called, and few are chosen. As believers, we are all called to be priests who stand in a place of authority and responsibility before God. Some are also chosen to help these priests. Larry Lea seems to be one of these chosen ones.

B.J. Willhite
Washington, D.C.
February 1991

ONE

CALLED TO
SOMETHING NEW

I answered God's call to be a praying priest when I was twenty-seven years old. It was 1978. I was the youth pastor of the three-thousand-member Beverly Hills Baptist Church in Dallas, Texas.

Once a year for five consecutive years the pastor, Howard Conatser, had called me into his office and given me the same speech. "Larry," he would drawl in his deep, raspy voice, "success without a successor is a failure. You are God's choice to be pastor of this church when I go off the scene. You are my 'Timothy,' so finish your education. Get prepared!"

Then in 1978 the doctors discovered that Pastor Conatser had cancer. We all fasted and wrestled in prayer for him. We thought we were winning the battle. One day, however, while I was visiting my parents in Kilgore, Texas, the phone rang. "Larry," a voice said, "Howard Conatser was just taken to the hospital."

I'll never forget what happened next. I immediately went to prayer for my beloved friend. As I rebuked the cancer and claimed healing, a familiar voice spoke in my spirit. It was as if someone had dropped a precious piece of crystal, shattering it into a thousand pieces: "Howard Conatser will die," the voice said softly, "and you will be refused as pastor of the church."

Within ten weeks Howard Conatser was dead.

When I met with the church board to discuss the future, they said they were willing for me to be their pastor as long as I was willing to preach fiery sermons and take big offerings; as long as a steady stream of people walked the aisle in response to the Sunday-morning invitations. But they didn't want to release me to continue leading the people toward the New Testament vision for the church that Pastor Conatser and I had shared.

To keep peace and prevent a church split, I resigned. Talk about a step down! I felt as if I were free-falling into a black, bottomless pit of obscurity. I moved my wife and children back to my hometown in east Texas, became an evangelist and started preaching in *big* places—like Arp, Texas.

Suddenly almost everything I valued was in my yesterdays. Fighting an internal war over what *should* have been, *might* have been or *could* have been, I sought God's face as never before.

10

Like Paul...what things were gain to me, I had to count as loss for Christ.

I was praying one evening in Los Angeles when the Lord spoke in my spirit and told me to read Isaiah 43:18-19. I opened my Bible and read these words:

> Do not remember the former things,
> Nor consider the things of old.
> Behold, I will do a new thing,
> Now it shall spring forth;
> Shall you not know it?
> I will even make a road in the wilderness
> And rivers in the desert.

Then God said to me, "If you want to find the new thing, you must release the past." My past had been good, but, like Paul in Philippians 3:7, what things were gain to me, I had to count as loss for Christ. God was calling me to let go of all my past successes, connections and opportunities. I released it all—the good and the bad, giving it to Jesus.

What did God do? He kept His promise. He gave me a new walk with Him and a new message.

When I had moved my family home to Kilgore, I knew God was sending me there to answer a call that was higher than the call to preach: It was the call to pray, and I heeded that call under the wing of Bob Willhite, pastor of the local Assembly of God church. For more than thirty years Pastor Willhite had persistently practiced the very thing for which my heart had been crying out—a consistent, daily prayer life.

He and I teamed up: Every morning the rising sun found us at his church, lying on our faces before God, crying out to Him for anointing and direction. As I responded to God's calling, He revealed to me how to pray based upon the Lord's prayer.

Armed with a new message, I preached at youth revivals and evangelized all over the United States and Canada. As I continued to rise early each morning to seek God's face, I eagerly shared the life-changing, soul-shaping revelation on how to pray.

Then God also gave me a new ministry. I was holding a revival in Canada when the voice of the Lord again spoke in my spirit: "Go to Rockwall and establish My people there." That's how it came about that in 1980 thirteen people and I, as pastor, founded Church on the Rock in Rockwall, Texas. God subsequently called me to raise up a 300,000-member nation-wide prayer army so that the judgments pronounced against our land might be turned and destruction averted.

The miraculous changes in my life and ministry never could have happened if I had not done two things: (1) released the past and (2) answered the call to pray.

Leaving the Old for the New

The apostle Paul, who knew all about change, wrote:

> But we all, with open face beholding as in a glass the glory of the Lord, are *changed* into the same image *from glory to glory*, even as by the Spirit of the Lord (2 Cor. 3:18, KJV, italics mine).

---

*If you don't want to be changed
again and again, stay away
from Jesus. He loves you too much
to leave you as you are.*

That Greek word translated "changed" is *metamorphoumetha*, from which we get the word *metamorphosis*. Metamorphosis describes the process by which tadpoles lose their tails, grow legs and become frogs; it's the course by which caterpillars become butterflies. Metamorphosis involves a change into another form. Paul, in 2 Corinthians 3:18, describes believers as being changed, "metamorphosed," by the power of the Holy Spirit, into Christ's image from glory to glory.

If you don't want to be changed again and again, stay away from Jesus. He loves you too much to leave you as you are. The process isn't always pleasant. Paul says we are changed into Christ's image "from glory to glory." He also says in Romans 1:17 that the righteousness of God is revealed "from faith to faith." Faith and glory sound wonderful, don't they? But there's something we need to understand about all this.

Between each level of faith and each level of glory there is always a cross, a surrender of self, a dying. The tadpole has to be willing to change if he's going to become a frog. The caterpillar must be willing to give up being what he has always been, spin a cocoon around himself and wait until he's fashioned into a butterfly. Similarly, we must be willing to die to the past; we must expect and accept God's new thing. We must become dead to what we used to be if we are ever to become something new. That is the secret to successful change.

13

Most of the Jewish leaders of Jesus' day didn't know that secret. They trusted in their traditions (the way they had *always* done things) and missed the Messiah. Their theological interpretation had become so rigid that they were unable to accept the new thing God was about to do in their midst.

They chose physical symbols over the invisible realities they symbolized. Jesus offered them a spiritual temple, but they wanted a physical temple. Jesus talked about an invisible kingdom, but they were interested only in an earthly, political kingdom. Jesus offered them power over the devil, but the Jews wanted power over the Romans. They weren't ready to release their expectations of God's plans for them. They didn't want any part of God's new thing.

Change makes stiffer demands on some of us than on others. For example, it was one thing for me, a twenty-seven-year-old youth pastor, to obey God's call to leave Dallas, pack up my family and move to east Texas. But think of the courage demanded of Bob Willhite, a man of many years' experience in denominational ministry, when God asked him to fold up his tent: He was pastoring an eight-hundred-member church in northwest Arkansas—a church he had birthed—when God commanded him to move to tiny Kilgore and pastor a church of about 250. That's where he was when God told me to move home to Kilgore and answer the call to pray.

When I met Pastor Willhite he asked me to hold a revival in his church. When we started praying, God sent us a revival—such a revival that the established religious structure couldn't contain it.

People, many of the "wrong" color, started getting saved. Some of the church leaders didn't like that nor did they like some of the other things the Holy Spirit was instructing Pastor Willhite to do. Several of his wealthy members were determined

---

*Change makes
stiffer demands on
some of us
than on others.*

---

to control their pastor and church.

But right then God saw fit to send a furloughed missionary to the church as a special speaker. Although the man had no knowledge of what was going on, he took his text from Judges 17 and talked about the priest that Micah bought—a preacher whose ministry was for sale to the highest bidder.

At the end of the sermon the missionary turned to Pastor Willhite and said, "I don't know what this means, but God tells me that you have a word for the congregation. You'd better obey God."

Pastor Willhite walked to the pulpit and said, "I want you people to know that from this point on I'm not going to take a penny from you. I'm giving my salary back to the church."

When the wealthy men could no longer exert control through finances, they said to Pastor Willhite, in so many words, "You can go, and you can take your boy (meaning me) with you." Because Bob Willhite was willing to obey God and let go of the past, he now heads the Prayer Embassy in Washington, D.C., helping to lead an international prayer revival. And do you know what? He's still open to change.

We shouldn't get too comfortable with our safe careers and secure schedules. When God says, "Get out of the nest and fly!" we'd better start flapping our wings.

After Oral Roberts spoke in our church for the first time, my son, John Aaron, came to me and asked: "Daddy, is Oral

Roberts old? He said he celebrated his sixty-eighth birthday this year. Is that old?"

"No, son," I answered. "Oral Roberts isn't old. You see, you're not old until you start living your life in the past. Even though Oral Roberts has lived sixty-eight years, he's still looking toward the future."

As I said that I remembered the devastated, disillusioned Larry Lea who left Beverly Hills Baptist Church. I wasn't yet thirty, but I was an old man inside because I was living my life in the past. Thank God I released the good and bad of my past and answered the call to prayer.

Are you "old"? Are you living your life in the past? Are you grieving over what might have been, should have been? Release it all to God. Answer the call to be a praying priest.

Ask Bob Willhite. Ask me. That next step may seem like a long way down, but in His time God will lift you up. He will make a road in your wilderness and cause rivers to run in your desert. He will do a *new* thing.

Standing in God's Ways

Every church and every believer must seek God for today and move in the mainstream of the Spirit's flow. Substituting reputations, programs or traditions for the fresh, surging stream of God's Spirit is a sure sign of declining spiritual health. Instead of cherishing and following the move of the Spirit, we may, through our programs and traditions, be dictating to God, telling Him what He can and cannot do.

In 1860 Andrew Murray—the beloved spiritual leader and author from South Africa known for his doctrine of holiness and his practical Christianity—fell into a trap of dictating to God. As the story is related in *The Pentecostals: The Charis-*

16

"You're not old until you start living your life in the past."

---

matic Movement in the Churches by W.J. Hollenweger, following one Sunday evening worship service, sixty young people from the church Murray pastored gathered in a small room; after singing a hymn and reading from Scripture, four or five young people took turns leading in prayer.

In the middle of one girl's stirring intercession, a distant rushing sound was heard. It came nearer and nearer until the room seemed to shake, and then suddenly nearly every young person present began to pray simultaneously, some in whispers, others in normal tones.

In the staid, well-ordered Presbyterian surroundings, the voices of some sixty people praying at once seemed almost deafening. An elder who heard the sound and saw what was going on rushed to call the pastor. Entering the room, Murray called out for silence; the praying continued. Again Murray cried: "People, I am your minister, sent from God. Silence!" Being so earnest in their intercession for mercy and pardon, the young people did not hear him.

After several more vain attempts to halt the proceedings, Andrew Murray said sternly, "God is a God of order, and here everything is in disorder." Then he left the meeting.

Every evening that week Murray himself held prayer meetings, and the crowd grew so large that they had to move to another building. He tried—unsuccessfully—to lead the prayer meeting along a quiet, subdued path.

17

Then on Saturday evening, as Murray led the meeting, the mysterious sound was again heard, drawing nearer and nearer. Just as before, the entire congregation plunged into simultaneous intercession.

When Murray called upon the group to be silent, a stranger who had been watching the proceedings from the doorway walked up to the agitated pastor and cautioned, "Be careful what you do, for the Spirit of God is at work here. I have just come from America, and this is precisely what I witnessed there."

As Murray heeded the stranger's warning, fifty young men offered themselves for the ministry, and the revival spread outward to the community and to surrounding towns.[1]

Like Andrew Murray, we tend to be afraid of what we have not experienced. We draw back from what we do not understand.

"If *that* is what consecration means," some say, backing away lest a drop of blood fall upon their comfortable habits, "I don't want to be consecrated." "If *that* is the anointing," others sniff piously, pointing at the glistening, oozing oil, "don't pour any of the stuff on me. If you don't mind, Lord, I prefer to stay within the secure boundaries of my dignified traditions."

But the life of Jesus goes nowhere without the touch of His blood. And the blessing and power of His Spirit move only where the anointing oil is allowed to flow with free course. It's true for denominations, institutions, churches and individual believers. If we are going to be followers of Jesus, we cannot be like those who cling to the old familiar ways. What God said to me applies to us all: If you want to find the new thing, you must release the past.

TWO

YOU ARE
A PRIEST

Believers in Jesus Christ have been chosen by God for a unique purpose. We have extraordinary privileges and exciting responsibilities that far supersede showing up on Sunday morning to critique platform performance or collect our blessings. We are priests of the most high God. Is that hard to believe—that every Christian is a priest?

At the beginning of human history every individual offered personal sacrifices and served as a priest before God. Each person could go directly to God with no advocate, no intermediary (see Gen. 4:3-5, for example). Later, when the children of Abraham were slaves of the Egyptians, the head of each family acted as priest on behalf of all household members. In Exodus 12, for example, each Hebrew father was instructed to slay a lamb and sprinkle its blood on the doorposts of his home so the death angel would pass over that house.

But after the children of Israel left Egypt, God's method of dealing with His people changed dramatically. Three months into their journey toward Canaan, their leader, Moses, in obedience to the Lord's direct command, brought the people out of the camp to meet with God. Standing at the foot of smoke-shrouded Mount Sinai, the nation trembled at the terrifying scene unfolding before their eyes.

As the Lord descended in fire, the mountain quaked violently. Huge clouds of smoke spiraled upward (Ex. 19:18-19; 20:18). Amid the blast of an unseen trumpet God spoke to Moses in an audible voice. Fleeing in terror, the people begged Moses, "You speak with us, and we will hear; but let not God speak with us, lest we die" (Ex. 20:19).

Verse 21 sums it up: "So the people stood afar off, but Moses drew near the thick darkness where God was." The Israelites, conscious only of their unworthiness, unable to endure God's holy presence, drew back. But Moses, who was intimately aware of God's character and nature, drew near. Believing Moses to be more acceptable to a holy God than they were, the Israelites wanted Moses to intervene and become their mediator before God.

But God had intended to make the entire nation a holy priesthood. Just three days before, God had given Moses this

20

---

*But God had intended to make the
entire nation a holy priesthood....They
were to become God's earthly instruments
of healing and reconciliation.*

---

message to deliver to the people:

> Now therefore, if you will indeed obey My voice and
> keep My covenant, then you shall be a special *treasure*
> to Me above all people.... And you shall be to Me *a
> kingdom of priests and a holy nation* (Ex. 19:5-6,
> italics mine).

Israel was chosen, set apart by God. He promised in Exodus
19:5 that Israel would be His *treasure*. The Hebrew word used
here refers to a king's treasure box reserved for his most
precious possessions. All the earth is God's, yet He chose Israel
above all other people and nations to be His own precious,
carefully guarded treasure. Israel was set apart for Jehovah as
His own. They were intended to be a holy kingdom of priests
who possessed the privilege of drawing near to God Himself.

As priests, the Israelites were called to minister to the Lord
and to function as mediators between God and sinful, needy
people. They were to become God's earthly instruments of
healing and reconciliation; through Israel, all the people of the
earth would be blessed (Gen. 12:3).

Levites as Substitutes

Immediately after the awesome events witnessed by all of

21

Israel at Mount Sinai, Moses went up into the mountain to receive God's Law for His covenant people (see Ex. 24-28). During this time God chose one tribe, the tribe of Levi, to be separated to minister before Him. He chose one man from this tribe, Aaron, to become Israel's high priest, and He commanded that Aaron's sons be installed to serve the people as priests.

Although God had claimed the firstborn males of all twelve tribes when He had spared them from the death angel (Ex. 13:11-16), He allowed the men from the tribe of Levi to become substitutes for their fellow tribesmen (Num. 3:9-13; 8:14-19).

The Aaronic priesthood was selected to offer up the people's prayers, thanksgivings and sacrifices to God and to convey God's mercy, salvation and blessing to the people. From this point on, each Israelite was to bring an offering to a specified place where a Levite would represent his family before God.

But the sad day came when the people of Israel, along with their priests, their prayers and their sacrifices, became a source of deep disappointment to God. In their rebellion and iniquity, they flagrantly disregarded the Lord's holy purposes.

"Your sacrifices aren't offerings from the heart!" God thundered. "They're nothing more than hollow, religious ceremony. I have had enough of your offensive offerings without obedience and your sanctimonious sacrifices without righteousness. I didn't invite your unholy feet to trample My courts. My ears will no longer hear your prayers because your hands are full of blood" (see Is. 1:11-17).

God made it clear what measures Israel would have to take if they wanted to have their broken relationship with Him restored. The nation would have to wash itself and put away its evil doings. The priests would have to be righteous intermediaries between God and mankind. In short, the people of Israel

---

*God...intended their priesthood to be a
service and a testimony to the rest of the
world. But gradually they moved further
and further away from God's intention.*

---

and their priests were to repent and return to their original
purpose. God commanded that they be ambassadors, caring for
and ministering to the needy and broken people of the world.

Remember, God had intended for the whole nation to be
priests, not only a selected few; He intended their priesthood
to be a service and a testimony to the rest of the world. But
gradually they moved further and further away from God's
intention.

The Priestly Ministry of Christ

We must understand that Old Testament priests were only a
type, a shadow of Jesus, the great High Priest who was to come.
The sacrifices Aaronic priests offered were mere symbols of
Jesus, God's Lamb who would take away the sin of the world.

Because Old Testament sacrifices were only a temporary
remedy for sin and could never make the people who offered
them perfect, the people and their priests were obliged to offer
the same sacrifices year after year (Heb. 10:1).

By the time Jesus was born, the Jews were still confused
about the purpose God had for them. While striving to be a
holy, separated people, the scribes and Pharisees substituted
religiosity for obedience, legalism for love. To be holy, according to the tradition of the Pharisees, you had to devote all your
time to endless regulation. Consequently, access to God was

out of reach for the common man.

Jesus made the following pronouncement to the Jewish leaders: "The kingdom of God will be taken from you and given to a nation bearing the fruits of it" (Matt. 21:43). Who was the nation to whom Christ referred? It was to be those who would believe in the Lord Jesus and carry His gospel to the world. Peter, one of Christ's original twelve apostles, explained this in a letter to persecuted Christians scattered around Asia Minor:

> But you are a chosen generation, a royal priesthood, a holy nation, His own special people, that you may proclaim the praises of Him who called you out of darkness into His marvelous light; who once were not a people but are now the people of God (1 Pet. 2:9-10).

Israel neglected her obligation to be God's instrument of healing and reconciliation. The best efforts of the Aaronic priesthood to fulfill that purpose were woefully inadequate (Heb. 10:1-4). But Jesus Christ, the Messiah, came to fulfill His ministry by offering up Himself. In every respect the priesthood of Jesus Christ surpassed that of the line of Aaron and fulfilled the priestly ministry that God had, from the beginning, ordained for Israel to manifest to the world.

After Christ's crucifixion, the ultimate sacrifice, there was no need for the animal sacrifices. His atoning death on the cross accomplished "a cleansing of sins" (Heb. 1:3, Amplified) that animal sacrifices could not. His sacrifice was more than a mere symbol, for when He, the Lamb of God, tasted death for every human (Heb. 2:9), the atonement was finished once and for all (Heb. 7:27; 9:26).

And what are our purposes as God's holy, royal priesthood?

You are a priest, called to be mankind's representative before God and God's representative before mankind.

Peter tells us: We are to "set forth the wonderful deeds and display the virtues and perfections of Him Who called us out of darkness into His marvelous light," and we are to "offer up [those] spiritual sacrifices [that are] acceptable and well-pleasing to God through Jesus Christ" (1 Pet. 2:9,5, Amplified).

As a believer you are called to the same priestly purposes as the nation of Israel: to minister unto the Lord in prayer and worship, to minister to others by demonstrating His power and goodness and to be an instrument through which the will of God might be done on earth as it is in heaven. You are a priest, called to be mankind's representative before God and God's representative before mankind.

As a priest of the most high God, you possess extraordinary privileges and exciting responsibilities. You can either welcome God's holy call, or, like Israel, you can renounce it.

I've made a tremendous discovery, one that has changed my life forever. I've discovered that Larry Lea is called to be more than a preacher or pastor or professor. Larry Lea is called to be a priest of the eternal, omnipotent, holy God. Like the Old Testament priests, I'm called to bring Him daily sacrifices. I'm called to bring God's message of reconciliation to desperate, broken people. I have a purpose in life that goes far beyond accumulating bricks and sticks and stuff—and so do you.

You too are a priest! You possess a divine call and purpose. You have sacred obligations and extraordinary privileges. The

25

call to prayer and praise as a priest of the most high God is a call to every New Testament believer. Don't follow the example of those who neglected God's purpose for themselves. Follow Jesus, who called you to be a priest—every one of you!

THREE

NO SPECTATOR PRIESTS

Who are you?" If you stood in the foyer of your church next Sunday and asked this question to members as they filed out after service, what sort of responses do you think you'd get? One member might say, "I'm a doctor." Another might say, "I'm a computer programmer." Someone else might say, "I'm a secretary." If I put the same question to you, what would *you* say?

Did you ever stop to think that what you do is not necessarily who you are? Your job is not what you are; it is simply what you do in order to support your priesthood. Whether you work with your head, your hands or your back, you are a priest. Until you understand this basic concept, you will scratch a "vocational itch" and wonder why your job is not fulfilling.

Christianity has become almost a spectator sport. Many believers seem to have developed this mind-set: I make a living, go to church and pay my tithes. The guys on the platform are the priests.

There is no way only the professional clergy could ever do what the entire people of God have been called to do. God appoints and plants apostles, prophets, evangelists, pastors and teachers that they might fully equip His people to spread the gospel and minister to one another. Then, as believers do the work of the ministry, the body of Christ is built up, and spiritual growth takes place. If we examine Ephesians 4:11-13 carefully, we discover this cause-and-effect relationship:

> And He Himself gave some to be apostles, some prophets, some evangelists, and some pastors and teachers, for the equipping of the saints for the work of ministry, for the edifying of the body of Christ, till we all come to the unity of faith and the knowledge of the Son of God, to a perfect man, to the measure of the stature of the fullness of Christ.

God never intended that the world would be reached by full-time, ordained ministers alone. Reaching the world is clearly the task of every believer, whether or not we happen to be ordained.

---

*Did you ever stop to think that what you do
is not necessarily who you are? Your job
is not what you are; it is simply what you
do in order to support your priesthood.*

Certainly almost every church finds it necessary to choose a qualified leader and to equip that person with the authority necessary to fulfill specified duties. They have found it necessary to remove from that person all or part of the burden of making a living in the secular world so that full time can be devoted to the service of the church (1 Cor. 9:14). The laity must understand, however, that they cannot pay a pastor to do what *they* have been called to do.

The pastor's sphere of service is primarily the church, whereas the laity's sphere of service is primarily the world. On their jobs and in their neighborhoods and communities the laity meet and minister to people whom their pastors will never meet. I know that's true because many of my own personal experiences bear it out. Here's one example.

I gave my heart to God when I was seventeen years old. About three years later, when I was a student at Dallas Baptist College, the Lord impressed upon my heart that I must walk in the Spirit and be sensitive to His promptings. One night while I was praying, an anointing came upon me, and I promised the Lord that I would try always to obey Him.

Within a day or so I was eating in a restaurant not far from the college when the Spirit of God spoke clearly to my heart: "When you walk out, I will show you a man to whom you are to talk."

I assumed the man would be someone my own age, a young

29

person whom I would feel comfortable approaching. He turned out to be an older man, sitting all alone, slumped over a table near the door with his head cradled in his hands, staring at a cup of coffee. I walked up to his table, hesitated just an instant, then walked right past him and out the door. I didn't know what to say. My mouth felt frozen.

I got in my car and started the engine, but the Spirit of God wouldn't leave me alone. "Are you going to do it or aren't you?" He asked. So I shut the motor off and went back inside.

Not waiting for an invitation or a friendly glance, I sat down at his table. "Sir," I said, "I've got to say something. I was so impressed to stop and speak to you."

Somewhat surprised but too despondent to protest, he replied, "What can you do to help me? I'm an alcoholic."

Little did he know that my dad had just been saved and delivered from alcohol about six weeks before. "Boy, do I have a story to tell you!" I exclaimed, plunging into my father's testimony. Within minutes I had led the man to Christ.

That's what I mean when I tell you that ordinary, individual believers meet desperate, needy people with whom their pastors will never come in contact. Christians encounter situations in life's "emergency rooms" that can't wait for one of the staff from the church to arrive on the scene. Sickness and sin and depression don't keep office hours. Death and desperation can't be put on hold. You and I must open our ears to the Spirit of God and obey Him when He prompts us to "speak a word in season to him who is weary" (Is. 50:4). We have the ministry, and God will hold us accountable for it.

Since every believer isn't an expert in church history, a brief historical overview might make this clergy/laity issue more clear.

A careful study of the book of Acts and the epistles reveals

30

The key to ministry and calling
[in the early church] seems to have
been the spiritual gifts which God
Himself gave to various believers.

---

that Christianity arose largely as a lay movement. The early church had little formal organization. In fact, the key to ministry and calling seems to have been the spiritual gifts which God Himself gave to various believers. It was understood that all the people of God were called to work for Him. The laity were active in their worship services (1 Cor. 14:16,26) and were involved in church discipline (James 5:16; 1 Cor. 5; Matt. 18:15-20).

At this time, the laity enjoyed full participation in teaching, missionary evangelism and instruction of new believers. An example would be Priscilla and her husband, Aquila, who were tent-makers. The couple had a church in their house (1 Cor. 16:19), helped the apostle Paul (Acts 18:18) and aided in the theological instruction of Apollos (v. 26). Healings, casting out of demons and the manifestation of spiritual gifts were common during the first hundred years of the church. Listen to this fascinating, second-century report from Irenaeus, taken from his work *Against Heresies*:

> For some do certainly and truly drive out devils, so that those who have thus been cleansed from evil spirits frequently both believe [in Christ] and join themselves to the church. Others have foreknowledge of things to come: they see visions, and utter prophetic expressions. Others still heal the sick by laying their

31

hands upon them, and they are made whole. Yea, moreover, as I have said, the dead even have been raised up and remained among us for many years. And what shall I more say? It is not possible to name the number of the gifts which the church, [scattered] throughout the world, has received from God, in the name of Jesus Christ, who was crucified under Pontius Pilate, and which she exerts day by day for the benefit of the Gentiles, neither practicing deception upon any, nor taking any reward from them. For as she has received freely from God, freely does she also minister....[1]

Historical accounts of missionary preaching in the first three centuries reveal that medical missionary activities among their pagan neighbors were highly effective because the Christians healed more people than the heathen exorcists.

Gradually the laity abdicated its ministry, and the church became dominated by a hierarchy of clergy. By the end of the third century the church was no longer viewed as a charismatic (spiritually gifted) community in which all believers were ministers and priests. Instead, believers were divided—clergy and laity, sacred and secular, male and female. The idea that the kingdom of priests included all members of the body of Christ didn't mean much in practice.

By the fourth century no layman could administer the sacraments. No psalms written by individual lay Christians could be sung in church; the laity were expected to sit passively through the services.

By the fifth century lay ministries had diminished even further. Widows, even if educated, could not baptize or teach men, and it was understood that laymen were not to preach.

By the end of the third century the church was no longer viewed as a charismatic (spiritually gifted) community in which all believers were ministers and priests.

The layman who sought ordination had to work his way through an elaborate network of ecclesiastical offices before attaining the presbyterate.

The sixteenth-century Reformation inspired by Martin Luther attempted to restore the principle and practice of the priesthood of the believer. Among the many changes Luther instituted was the return of small groups—gatherings of believers, which he called "house churches."

John Wesley (1703-91), founder of the Methodist movement, carried on the house-church theme. He required three weekly meetings: a preaching meeting, a teaching meeting and a class meeting in which everyone shared what the Lord was doing in his or her own life.

Luther, Wesley and others who followed sought to restore the church to what it had been originally: a fellowship of believers, all actively participating in the work of the ministry. But as time passed, the laity again assumed a spectator mentality, and what should have been the work of all the people of God slowly became the task of a few—the professional clergy.

Today many Christians enter the church doors with a mind-set of "I'm coming to get my blessing" instead of "I'm coming to be a blessing." Instead of obeying Christ's command to visit the sick, apathetic Christians dial the church office. They tell the pastor that some sister is down on her back again, and by this they think they've done their duty.

As I have pointed out, pastors, even with paid professional support staff, cannot do what the laity have been called to do. Today we expect a pastor to implement effective programs, visit the sick, marry the love-smitten and bury the dead. Pastors must be counselors, administrators, teachers, fund-raisers, architects, janitors and worship leaders. We expect pastors to be motivators without becoming manipulators, to prepare inspiring messages and to win scores to Christ in spite of the fact that we allow them little time to study or pray.

What am I saying? There's much more to being a member of the family of God than showing up at the table two or three times a week to eat. If we're not carrying out our priestly responsibilities daily, we are only playing religious games.

I firmly believe that if we are to "turn the world upside down" for Christ as the early church did, we must understand three important New Testament principles:

• *All believers are called* (1 Pet. 2:9).
• *All believers are spiritually gifted* (1 Cor. 12:4-11; Rom. 12:4-8).
• *All believers are ministers* (1 Pet. 4:10,11; 1 Cor. 12:5; Acts 11:29).

That, in a nutshell, is the New Testament's theology of laity and clergy. Commissioned by the Lord Himself to be a kingdom of priests, all believers have a divine call and responsibility to perform their priestly duties and build up the body of Christ.

Now I want to ask a question: Who are you? I hope you don't state your occupation in reply; instead, I hope you square your shoulders and declare: "I am a priest of the most high God!"

FOUR

KNOWING THE HEART
AND MIND OF GOD

God is calling you to become a praying priest. In fact, God is calling out an enormous company of praying priests. He wants His people to become men and women of prayer and intercession. If we are not walking and living in prayer, we will be out of sync with what is going on in the kingdom of God.

To feel what is in God's heart and to understand what He has in His mind, you have to spend time in His presence.

A Spirit of Revelation

Until you accept God's call to be an intercessor and develop your own intimate relationship with Him, you will have little firsthand spiritual insight. You'll only mimic other men and women of God.

If you want God to speak to you, then you must begin speaking to Him on behalf of yourself and others. You must form the holy habit of ministering (*leitourgeo*) to the Lord, setting aside time for the sacred, priestly service that every believer can offer to God through prayer and personal adoration (Acts 13:2). As you do this, clear, refreshing revelation will flow out of your spirit.

Let me assure you that God wants to talk to you, even more than you want Him to talk to you. He's just waiting for you to get your priorities into proper order. That applies to preachers as much as it applies to their congregations.

Ninety-eight percent of what I preach comes to me while I'm in prayer. I sit or kneel in my study with my Bible nearby or in my hand. As I pray and listen to the Holy Spirit, God brings a word to my heart.

Many preachers go through the process backward. You see, in seminary we were taught to prepare a sermon methodically: study the Bible; get an idea; use the tools of exegesis, hermeneutics and homiletics to build a sermon around that idea; then pray and ask God to bless it.

I believe in studying the Bible. I follow a daily Bible-reading program and study God's Word systematically. I have served as the dean of the seminary at Oral Roberts University. I believe

Let me assure you that God wants to talk to you, even more than you want Him to talk to you. He's just waiting for you to get your priorities into proper order.

in education and diligent study.

But we pastors ought to pray until revelation is received, let that truth germinate in our spirits, study it out in the Word, pray and weep over it and then deliver that truth under the power and anointing of the Holy Spirit. When a preacher can stand and declare, "Thus saith the Lord to you today!" the voice within that preacher's voice will pierce people's hearts and propel them out of their complacency.

In times past God spoke to His people from the outside in. To hear from God, the ordinary person had to seek out a priest or prophet. But now He speaks from the inside out, through His Holy Spirit who dwells within us and communicates to and through our spirits.

Jesus, our great High Priest, promised:

> And I will pray the Father, and He will give you another Helper, that He may abide with you forever, even the Spirit of truth, whom the world cannot receive, because it neither sees Him nor knows Him; but you know Him, for He dwells with you and will be in you.... But the Helper, the Holy Spirit, whom the Father will send in My name, He will teach you all things, and bring to your remembrance all things that I said to you (John 14:16-17,26).

As a believer you should pray daily:

> For this reason we also, since the day we heard it, do
> not cease to pray for you, to ask that you may be filled
> with the knowledge of His will in all wisdom and
> spiritual understanding; that you may have a walk
> worthy of the Lord, fully pleasing Him, being fruitful
> in every good work and increasing in the knowledge
> of God (Col. 1:9-10).

God has given New Testament priests sources of guidance
and counsel in discerning His will. We have access to the Word
of God, to the Holy Spirit and to the revelation gifts of the
Spirit—the word of wisdom, the word of knowledge and
prophecy. As we daily put on our breastplates of righteousness
(Eph. 6:14) and keep our hearts sensitive and open, the voice
of the Holy Spirit will take the things of the Father and show
them to us. He will guide us into all truth.

Why do pastors and their people need such revelation? To
disclose the enemy's line of attack; to outline the spiritual
maneuvers that will destroy Satan's forces. Through revelation
the Spirit of God speaks clear, distinct directions and solutions
for our circumstances and problems, whatever they may be—
financial, physical, spiritual or emotional. Revelation is an
indispensable part of a praying priest's equipment.

After revelation, the praying priest needs the manifestation
of God's supernatural power. But such manifestation does not
come automatically. It depends on your courage—courage to
obey the revelation you have received, courage to hold onto it
and walk it out.

Think about the times you've failed spiritually. You probably
did so for one of two reasons: Without receiving revelation from

---

*A praying priest needs a spirit of
intercession, which leads to revelation.
Then revelation mixed with courage
to obey results in manifestation.*

---

the Lord, you went out presumptuously and said, "In the name
of Jesus I am going to do this if it kills me" (and it almost did).
Or, if you had received revelation, you didn't have enough
courage to hold fast to that word from God and follow it all the
way through. Courage is the missing link between revelation
and the manifestation of God's power.

Let's sum it up. A praying priest needs a spirit of *intercession*,
which leads to *revelation*. Then *revelation* mixed with courage
to obey results in *manifestation*. God still promises: "Call to
Me, and I will answer you, and show you great and mighty
things, which you do not know" (Jer. 33:3). Only God knows
the mighty exploits that can be accomplished in the days ahead
by the people who choose to spend time before Him in
intercession, receive His revelation, courageously obey it and
see supernatural manifestation.

Feeling the Heart of God

"Dr. Lea! Dr. Lea!"
"What now?" I mumbled under my breath that crisp fall
morning in 1988. I was trying to wear two hats—pastor of
Church on the Rock in Rockwall and dean of the ORU Graduate
School of Theology in Tulsa. I already had a dozen things to
take care of before catching a late afternoon flight from Tulsa
back to Texas.

I heaved a sigh as I looked down the crowded, narrow hall bustling with ORU students hurrying to their next classes and saw the man who had called out my name. He was sitting in a wheelchair waving something that looked like a note. I took a step in his direction, but somebody else grabbed my arm wanting to ask a question. I never got around to the young man in the wheelchair.

I made my way back to my office to finish preparing the sermon on compassion I was to preach that night at my church back in Rockwall. But I couldn't concentrate. Something kept gnawing at the back of my mind. What was it? What had I forgotten?

Then I remembered the man in the wheelchair. It was as if God said, "Son, until you get his note and minister to him, you have no business standing up before your congregation tonight and preaching on compassion." So I called one of the secretaries, described the man to her, asked her to find him—and his note.

She brought me the note, and it read something like this: "Dear Dr. Lea, I've asked Phyllis to marry me. She's probably my only real chance to be married. I've prayed so hard about this, but I've laid it at the feet of Jesus. No matter what God does, I'm still going to love Him, but I sure hope she says yes. She hasn't answered me yet, but would you pray? Can I depend upon you to pray for me?"

My heart went out to that lonely man whose life was on the line, and I cried out to God for him and for Phyllis.

Even though it wasn't written anywhere on that crumpled note, somehow between the lines I read another message. It said, "Dr. Lea, are you just a big shot running around these halls, or do you really care about people?"

I bowed my head and renewed a vow I'd made to God a long

> *But [an Old Testament priest]*
> *wasn't fully equipped to stand before a*
> *holy God on behalf of sinful people*
> *unless he had a compassionate heart.*

---

time ago. A vow about loving people. A vow about being a priest with a compassionate heart.

You see, an Old Testament priest might have been clothed in holy garments and consecrated. But he wasn't fully equipped to stand before a holy God on behalf of sinful people unless he had a compassionate heart that could weep with the sorrowful and rejoice with the joyful. An interceding priest had to be compassionate.

We're no different. Until we are baptized in compassion, we will never intercede effectively. We can learn all the prayer formulas. We can practice until we get the inflection in our voices just right. We can memorize everything anyone has to teach about prayer. But until we have compassionate hearts, we'll never be effective priests.

The Model of Compassion

Jesus was a model of compassion. When writing their Gospels, Matthew and Mark often chose the Greek word *splanchnizomai*, meaning "to be moved in one's inward emotions, to yearn with compassion," when describing Christ's reaction toward the multitudes and to individual sufferers.

As Jesus went through the cities and villages, curing all kinds of disease and every weakness and infirmity and preaching to the throngs, *"He was moved with pity and sympathy for them,* because they were bewildered—harassed and distressed and dejected and helpless—like sheep without a shepherd" (Matt. 9:36, Amplified, italics mine).

Matthew 14 relates the story of the death of John the Baptist. Upon hearing the news, heartbroken Jesus withdrew to a solitary place. When the desperate crowds followed Him, Jesus was not annoyed. Instead, *"He had compassion (pity and deep sympathy) for them* and cured their sick" (Matt. 14:14, Amplified, italics mine).

There was a progression in Jesus' actions. First, He saw the great throng. Next, He was moved with pity and deep sympathy for them. Then He cured their sick. As Jesus looked upon the people in their need, His compassionate heart overflowed with the desire to heal them.

You see, compassion is that something stirring inside you that says, I've got to do something about this. I can't sit back and do nothing. I've got to touch God for these people.

Christ's merciful ministry was simply the overflow of a compassionate heart in constant touch with the Father whose love had found a way to touch, redeem and heal a sin-stricken world. For years I've noticed that some people are driven to pray out of duty. Others pray with the hope of personal reward. But the compassionate heart of Jesus often drove Him to rise hours before dawn so He could seek His Father's face.

Sometimes we picture Jesus with righteous anger flashing in His eyes. There's a scourge in His hand, and He's driving bleating sheep, fluttering doves and greedy money-changers out of the temple. We forget that only minutes before that display of stern judgment Jesus had broken down and wept with compassion as He approached the city of Jerusalem (Luke 19:41).

Christ's grief was more than the easy shedding of a tear or

---

*Compassion is that something
stirring inside you that says, I've got
to do something about this...I've got
to touch God for these people.*

---

two. Luke chose the word *klaio* to describe Christ's weeping—a
word used for any loud expression of grief, especially in
mourning for the dead. It means "to break forth, to wail." This
same word is used to describe the way Peter wept and mourned
after denying Jesus (Luke 22:62).

Jesus poured out His grief for the city in audible wails and
sobs. He knew the time of God's gracious mercy toward
Jerusalem was short; the prophesied destruction of the city was
fast approaching.

Nor was this the only time that Jesus cried publicly. John
chose the word *dakruo*, meaning "to shed tears," to describe
Christ's visible grief when He saw Mary and her friends
sobbing over the death of her brother, Lazarus (John 11:35).
Seeing Christ's tears, the onlooking Jews whispered, "See how
tenderly He loved him!" (John 11:36, Amplified).

Where did we ever get the notion that "real" men, "macho"
men, don't cry? Man, as we know him, is only a perverted,
deformed shadow of the God of love in whose image he was
created. If we want to see what God is like, if we want to see
men and women as God intended them to be, we must look at
Jesus who is "the exact likeness of the unseen God—the visible
representation of the invisible" (Col. 1:15, Amplified).

Jesus shed tears. Jesus wept. Why? Because He was filled
with compassion, and compassion must do something to relieve
a person's problems or pains. Compassion must cry out to God

on behalf of others.

In your circles of influence, as in mine, suffering abounds. Our pity and sympathy aren't enough. If you and I are to make a difference, we must have hearts that yearn and throb with Christlike compassion, and that compassion must drive us to intercession.

Compassion takes the time to get involved. Compassion labors and sweats. Compassion gets dirty. Compassion is acquainted with grief, bears the sorrows, suffers the agonies and is touched by the feelings of others' infirmities. Compassion cares enough to invest precious hours in intercession before God for the hurting, needy and even for the rebellious.

FIVE

INTERCEDING AT THE ALTAR OF INCENSE

Intercession was an integral part of the Old Testament priests' ministry. Morning and evening a priest was to stand in the holy place before the altar of incense, representing the needs of the people and communing with God.

In the courtyard outside the tabernacle stood the brass altar of burnt offering—a place of sacrifice and suffering, a place for sinners. This altar was a solemn witness that without the shedding of blood there was no access to God and no forgiveness of sin.

But inside the tabernacle in the holy place, centered directly before the veil guarding the awesome holy of holies, was another altar, the altar of incense (Ex. 30:6; 40:5). The small, golden altar stood in the direct line of the high priest's approach to the mercy seat, where God's presence dwelt behind the veil. Only cleansed, consecrated priests had access to the altar of incense; no sinner could approach it.

Upon this altar the priest offered a special kind of incense prescribed by God Himself. Each morning when the golden lamps were refilled and trimmed, and again at evening when the lamps were lighted, a priest clad in clean white linen approached the altar of burnt offering and filled a golden bowl with burning coals from the altar. Taking the coals and a golden censer of fragrant incense, he reverently entered the holy place and placed the glowing coals upon the altar. Then he liberally applied the powdered incense. Soon billows of perfumed smoke filled the holy place and the holy of holies.

In both the Old and New Testaments, incense is the symbol of the prayers of the righteous. The psalmist cried:

Let my prayer be set before You as incense, the lifting
up of my hands as the evening sacrifice (Ps. 141:2).

John, the beloved apostle, spoke of incense as representing the prayers of God's people. In describing his glorious vision of heaven, he said:

Then another angel, having a golden censer, came and
stood at the altar. And he was given much incense,

> *God's Word makes it clear that our prayers delight the Lord, ascending like clouds of fragrant incense to His very throne.*

that he should offer it with the prayers of all the saints upon the golden altar which was before the throne. And the smoke of the incense, with the prayers of the saints, ascended before God from the angel's hand (Rev. 8:3-4).

God's Word makes it clear that our prayers delight the Lord, ascending like clouds of fragrant incense to His very throne. We must not allow a sense of unworthiness or feelings of apathy to prevent our coming before God each day to render a sweet-smelling offering of prayer.

The Two Altars of New Testament Priests

As a believer your body is the temple, the very sanctuary of the Holy Spirit who lives in you (1 Cor. 6:19). Within the sanctuary of your spirit are two altars, each with its own distinct purpose.

First is the altar of burnt offering, the altar on which we present ourselves and our service to God. Our sacrifices are necessary and pleasing to God, but they are not all God wants of us. Service and sacrifice are not substitutes for prayer. All our labors and sacrifices for God cannot take the place of communion with Him at the altar of incense. He desires our fellowship and our sweet-smelling prayers and praises. If we are to be whole, joyful Christians maintaining the proper balance between duty and devotion, we must take time each day to minister before the Lord at both altars.

The altar of incense symbolizes prayer and communion between us and God. We see represented in it Christ's intercession for us and also our prayers and intercessions in His name.

Jesus Christ, our Savior and example, was and still is an intercessor. All through His earthly ministry Jesus went from one place of prayer to the next place of prayer; in between, He worked miracles.

He interceded all night before choosing His disciples. He prayed at His baptism. He withdrew from the crowds and prayed. He often rose long before daybreak and sought the face of His heavenly Father. He prayed and opened blind eyes. He prayed, then walked on water. He prayed and multiplied five loaves and two fishes to feed five thousand famished people. He prayed, then healed the brokenhearted and set Satan's captives free. In the Garden of Gethsemane He prayed. He prayed on the cross. Even now, in heaven, He is making intercession for us (Heb. 7:25).

Jesus appears in the presence of God on our behalf. There, at the Father's right hand, Jesus makes petition to God, interceding and intervening for mankind. I am on His prayer list, and so are you.

And as if that were not enough, Jesus has also given us the Holy Spirit to come to our aid and bear us up in our weaknesses. When we do not know how to pray as we ought, the Holy Spirit pleads on our behalf with unspeakable yearnings and groanings too deep for utterance, praying in perfect harmony with God's will (Rom. 8:26-27).

Understanding God's gracious provision, the writer of Hebrews issued this joyful invitation: "Let us therefore come

---

If we are to be whole, joyful Christians maintaining the proper balance between duty and devotion, we must take time to minister before the Lord at both altars.

---

boldly to the throne of grace, so that we may obtain mercy and find grace to help in time of need" (Heb. 4:16).

Jesus Christ, our great High Priest, has invited us to participate with Him in the ministry of intercession. He taught us that "men ought always to pray and not lose heart" (Luke 18:1). He said, "Ask, and it will be given you; seek, and you will find; knock, and it will be opened to you" (Matt. 7:7). He declared that some things can come forth by nothing but prayer and fasting (Mark 9:29). Jesus promised that "if two of you agree on earth concerning anything that they ask, it will be done for them" (Matt. 18:19), and that all things, whatever we ask in prayer, believing, we will receive (Matt. 21:22).

After This Manner, Pray

But Jesus did not command us simply to offer up the incense of prayer; He also taught us how. The Old Testament priests offered only the incense specified by God; none other was appropriate. Our prayers should also be made according to His specifications. When the disciples asked Jesus to teach them to pray, He said:

> After this manner therefore pray ye: Our Father which art in heaven, Hallowed be thy name. Thy kingdom come. Thy will be done in earth, as it is in heaven.

Give us this day our daily bread. And forgive us our debts, as we forgive our debtors. And lead us not into temptation, but deliver us from evil: For thine is the kingdom, and the power, and the glory, for ever. Amen (Matt. 6:9-13, KJV).

Years ago in desperation I asked God to teach me how to pray. I had such a great desire to know God and to commune with Him, but I felt as if I were drying up and perishing spiritually because I didn't know how to pray. One day as I was crying out to God again, begging Him to teach me how to pray, He pointed me to the familiar prayer in Matthew 6 that we have come to know as the Lord's prayer.

"But, God," I protested, "I can say that in thirty seconds and sing it in a minute and a half."

The Lord replied, "Say it real s-l-o-w."

So I obeyed. "Our...Father...which...art...in...heaven," I repeated very slowly, pausing at the end of each word, "Hallowed...be...Thy...name."

At this point the Lord showed me a wonderful vision. I saw Jesus holding a big basin in His hands. I watched in awe as He walked to an altar and poured out the basin's contents—His own blood. As He did so, the swirling, living mass of Christ's precious blood upon the altar began to testify, explaining what Jesus has provided for me through the new covenant.

"Because of the blood of Jesus, your sins are forgiven and you can approach the presence of God. You are the righteousness of God in Christ for He is *Jehovah-tsidkenu*, the Lord Your Righteousness. Sin shall not have dominion over you, for He is *Jehovah-m'kaddesh*, the Lord Your Sanctifier.

"You can experience His abiding presence and the fullness of the Holy Spirit. He is with you and in you, for He is

---

We can enter the presence of God in prayer by reflecting upon who God is for us and by thanking Him for all that the blood of Jesus has purchased for us.

Jehovah-shammah, the Lord Who Is There. Your heart and mind can be filled with the peace of God, for He is *Jehovah-shalom*, the Lord Your Peace.

"You can live in physical, mental and emotional soundness," the testifying blood continued, "for by His stripes you were healed. He is *Jehovah-rophe*, the Lord Your Healer.

"You can experience success, for Christ has redeemed you from the curse of the law. He sees your needs beforehand and makes provision for them, for He is *Jehovah-jireh*, the Lord Whose Provision Shall Be Seen.

"You need not fear death or hell or any attack by the enemy, for He is *Jehovah-nissi*, the Lord Your Banner, and *Jehovah-rohi*, the Lord Your Shepherd."

By this time I was lost in the presence of God, caught up in thanksgiving for the blood of Christ. I was glorifying God, hallowing His beautiful names, when the Spirit of God reminded me that this was only the *first line of the prayer. I had only said hello, and there I was, lost in the presence of God.*

That's how I learned that we can enter the presence of God in prayer by reflecting upon who God is for us and by thanking Him for all that the blood of Jesus has purchased for us. Every day in prayer I've learned to come before God just as Jesus taught us to. I take time to bless His holy name and bask in His glorious presence, for if I need *anything*, I need *Him*.

That day back in 1978, as the series of visions continued, the

Lord showed me that the Lord's prayer is actually a prayer outline in which Jesus gives six topics as a pattern to follow and elaborate upon under the guidance of the Holy Spirit. These six topics cover every area of our prayer needs.

"After this manner therefore pray ye," instructed Jesus. If Jesus suddenly appeared before you today, looked you in the eyes and said, "When you pray, do it My way. Here's the way to approach the Father and to bring your needs before Him," wouldn't you at least try it? Then why insist on trying to pray some other way instead of learning to pray as He taught?

God's priests must not offer up strange incense to Him but learn to pray in obedience to His command.

The Protocol of the Priesthood

In September 1986 six other people and I were invited to a meeting and lunch with a United States senator. The first thing I noticed was the protocol—the rules of etiquette and specified procedures. The senator and his aides had their own terminology and used a kind of political, ambassadorial language to which I was unaccustomed.

I'm usually pretty relaxed when I meet new people, but this time Larry Lea was careful to do everything properly. First of all, I didn't wear my old blue jeans. I didn't slap the senator on the back or call him by his first name. I didn't chew gum. The temptation to rear back in my chair and prop up my feet on his desk never even entered my mind. I said "Yes, Senator" and "No, Senator." When I left his office that day and he said, "I want you to do some things for me," I replied, "Yes, sir."

New Testament priests also have a certain protocol to follow. We dress appropriately in our supernatural, priestly garments. We come to God only one way—through the blood of Jesus.

Jesus, our elder Brother, has taught us the protocol of priestly prayer—what we should say, how we should pray—when we approach our heavenly Father.

We enter God's presence with thanksgiving and give praise to His name. We use the right words when we bow before Him. When we walk out the door, we follow through on what He has told us to do. That's what I mean by the protocol of the priesthood.

Jesus, our elder Brother, has taught us the protocol of priestly prayer—what we should say, how we should pray—when we approach our heavenly Father. He has also provided an ambassadorial language of the kingdom—a prayer language of the Spirit—that we may use when our limited, natural language is insufficient to express what's in our hearts or when we do not know how to pray as we ought.

In my book *Could You Not Tarry One Hour?* I teach readers how to pray, using the Lord's prayer as a model. But just in case you haven't had the opportunity to study the Lord's prayer in detail with me, the following brief explanation will help you learn how to pray according to the model prayer Jesus gave us.

Promises

Our Father which art in heaven, Hallowed be thy name.

As a praying priest, begin your daily ministry with praise, hallowing and exalting the name of our Father. First, thank God for sending His Son to redeem you, for if it weren't for Jesus, you could not call God Father (Gal. 4:4-6).

Then hallow the name of God by agreeing with who our

Father is and what He has already done in Jesus Christ. Praise God for the promises He makes to His people under the new covenant—promises fulfilled in the person and work of Christ. Through praise you enter into the very presence of God, opening the way to bring your petitions before Him.

Priorities
Thy kingdom come. Thy will be done.

God's kingdom is established in you when you obey Him and accept His will and authority in your life. As your prayer proceeds, declare that God's kingdom of righteousness, joy and peace (Rom. 14:17) shall come and that His will and priorities shall be established in these four areas: (1) you, (2) your loved ones, (3) your church and (4) your nation. Pray over each of these areas specifically, one by one. God's kingdom must be first in your heart if you are to be His priest.

Provision
Give us this day our daily bread.

After you have given yourself to God's will and made His kingdom your priority, ask His provision for your physical and material needs. To receive God's provision, you must first *be in the will of God* (see Heb. 10:22,25; 1 John 1:7; Heb. 13:7,17; 1 Thess. 4:11-12; 2 Thess. 3:10-12; Mal. 3:10).

Second, you must claim God's promises and *believe it is God's will to prosper you,* for this will give you confidence to come daily before the Lord with your needs (see Matt. 6:33; James 1:6-7; Luke 6:38; Mark 10:29-30; Phil. 4:19).

Third, you must *be specific* (see Phil. 4:6; Matt. 6:11). Don't pray in generalities. Make definite requests.

Fourth, *be tenacious* (see Dan. 10:12-14; Matt. 7:7, Amplified; Luke 18:1; Heb. 11:6). Keep praying until your answer

---

In prayer each day make up your mind how you are going to treat people. Remember that you are a priest with the purpose of ministering God's love and mercy to others.

---

comes. Refuse to let discouragement or unbelief rob you of your answers to prayer.

 People

Forgive us our debts as we forgive our debtors.

If you want to get along with people, you must ask God to forgive your wrong relationships, attitudes and so on. You must forgive and release others if you want God to forgive you and remove your sin, guilt and tormenting memories.

In prayer each day make up your mind how you are going to treat people. Remember that you are a priest with the purpose of ministering God's love and mercy to others. Make the decision in your will that you will love people even if they hate you and that you will not allow anything or anybody to steal your peace and your joy.

Power

And lead us not into temptation, but deliver us from evil.

At the beginning of every day, as an interceding priest, you should pray a hedge of protection about yourself, your loved ones and your possessions. Psalm 91 gives three reasons why you can claim God's protection: (1) because you have made the Lord your habitation, or dwelling place (v. 9); (2) because you have set your love upon Him (v. 14); and (3) because you have known His name (v. 14). Make certain each day that you are

55

doing these three things so that you will experience God's protection.

As your defense against the wiles of the devil, put on the whole armor of God, piece by piece, as outlined in Ephesians 6:14-17, believing and declaring that Jesus is your armor of light (Rom. 13:12,14). These are the spiritual garments of your priesthood.

Fully clad in the armor of God and encircled by His hedge of protection, you can stand secure in the victory Jesus has won for you. You can fight the good fight of faith and defeat the powers of darkness.

 Praise

For thine is the kingdom, and the power, and the glory for ever. Amen.

The Lord's prayer begins and ends with praise. As you come to this last prayer topic, praise God because He has invited you to be a partaker of His kingdom (2 Tim. 4:18; Luke 12:32), His power (Ps. 68:35; Luke 10:19) and His glory (2 Cor. 3:18; Heb. 2:9-10). God's priests should never enter or leave God's presence without humbly bowing before Him and offering a sweet-smelling sacrifice of praise.

Desire, Discipline and on to Delight

As you begin praying as Jesus taught His disciples to pray, you will be amazed at the dramatic increase in the effectiveness of your prayer ministry and the deepening of your relationship with the Lord.

You will also realize that discipline does not come from the outside in, but from the inside out. As the Spirit of God teaches you how to pray and plants within you a desire to pray, the desire

> *The more time I spend in God's presence, the more I realize that prayer is the greatest of our ministries. Prayer is the holiest work of all.*

and revelation work outward in discipline. Then discipline carries you to holy delight. Prayer becomes the delight of your life.

The Most Sacred Service

The most honorable and sought-after service in the daily ministry of Old Testament priests was burning the incense on the golden altar within the holy place. They actually drew lots for the privilege. It should be so for New Testament priests as we learn to perform the delightful, holy work of prayer.

The more time I spend in God's presence, the more I realize that prayer is the greatest of our ministries. Prayer is the holiest work of all.

When I wake up each morning, my heart is already yearning to enter God's presence. The sacred fire awaits my sacrifice. The golden lamps flicker and smoke, ready to be trimmed and refilled with the oil of the Spirit. God waits, yearning for my communion, eagerly anticipating the sweet incense of prayer.

My soul runs to meet Him. Soon the inner sanctuary of my heart is filled with the perfume of praise. As I intercede, dangers are averted, and Satan's traps are sprung. Hearts are opened to truth. Burdens are lifted. Ministries are blessed. Bodies are strengthened and healed. Needs are met.

The fire burns. The incense rises. I press on, knowing that, if I let go, people who desperately need my intercession may succumb to Satan. Strategic pressure points can give way and be lost to the cause of Christ and the kingdom of God forever. I persevere, confident that the effective, fervent prayer of the righteous avails much (James 5:16).

I rise from my knees, but God's presence goes with me. All through the day I offer up my thoughts, words and works as a sacrifice to Him. I hear His words of counsel. I receive His words of correction. I draw strength from Him. I dwell in the secret place of the Most High. I wear garments of praise that are fragrant with the scent of incense. And wherever the tasks of the day carry me, I am conscious that His presence makes holy ground.

Never forget. Service and sacrifice should never preempt prayer. A gleaming, golden altar stands waiting in the sanctuary of your soul. Don't neglect it.

SIX

THE SIN
PROBLEM

God explicitly commanded: "The priests shall teach My people the difference between the holy and the common or profane, and cause them to distinguish between the unclean and the clean" (Ezek. 44:23, Amplified). You and I live in a day when the human race has lost the sense of the holiness of God and the seriousness of sin. To become what

Christ has called her to be, the church must recognize God's great demand for holiness and appreciate His abundant provision for it.

Confronting Sin

New Testament priests must confront sin on a daily basis: first in ourselves, then in others and in our nation. We must deal with our *own* sin if we want our prayers to make a difference and be heard on high, for it is "the effective, fervent prayer" of the *righteous* that avails much (James 5:16). The Word of God clearly warns that if we regard iniquity in our hearts, the Lord will not hear us (Ps. 66:18).

New Testament priests must deal with the sins of *others* by making intercession for the rebellious and restoring the fallen. We must earnestly warn the wicked, pleading with them to turn from their sin, or their blood will be upon our hands (Ezek. 3:18-21).

We must deal with the sins of our *nation*, for her very life and existence are in peril unless she repents, receives forgiveness and becomes reconciled to an offended, holy God.

As New Testament priests we need to learn a lesson of which Old Testament priests were continually reminded: Sin is serious!

In Old Testament worship no one could appear before God without an animal sacrifice, for sacrifice opened the way into God's presence. Because of that central act of worship, the smoking altar, a place of bloody death, dominated the tabernacle. It was the first object seen by the Jewish people and their priests as they entered the enclosed court surrounding the tabernacle.

As we study the Old Testament sacrifices, we will see that

60

All the sacrificial rituals—and even the arrangement of the tabernacle itself—were designed to reveal the distance between sinful humanity and a holy God.

---

all the sacrificial rituals—and even the arrangement of the tabernacle itself—were designed to reveal the distance between sinful humanity and a holy God.

The Tabernacle

The tabernacle was divided into two unequal chambers. The larger outer chamber, called the holy place, was separated from the outer court by a blue, purple and scarlet screen through which the common people dared not pass.

The innermost chamber of the Old Testament tabernacle, the most holy place or the holy of holies, was separated from the outer chamber, the holy place, by a magnificent, elaborately embroidered curtain called the veil. Beyond that veil in the holy of holies was the ark of the covenant, a gold-covered box just under four feet in length and about two feet in width and height. The mercy seat covered the ark, and hovering over the mercy seat was the *shechinah*, the visible, luminous cloud manifesting God's glorious presence.

Only the high priest could go beyond the veil. The other priests, the people's mediators and representatives, stood on the other side of the veil—the outside. Access to God's holy presence was limited to one man. Even the anointed high priest could approach the mercy seat and the awesome cloud of God's glory only once a year on the day of atonement. And on that day the high priest exposed himself to certain death if he dared enter God's presence and approach the mercy seat without the fragrant incense or the atoning blood of sacrifice that covered sin.

Outside the tabernacle, within the open courtyard, the people worshipped and presented sacrificial offerings. Near the center of the courtyard a great altar, measuring nearly eight feet square and five feet tall, was always open and accessible to any guilty Israelite. In the courtyard air, smoke from a miraculously kindled fire, tended by the priests and kept burning upon the brazen altar day and night, mingled with the odors of spilt blood and burning flesh.

The altar of sacrifice was a constant reminder that sin was costly and that forgiveness was not cheap. No Old Testament Jew or priest could be casual about sin or pretend that sin did not matter, for the blood of thousands of animal sacrifices that stained the altar served as a graphic reminder of sin's seriousness, man's desperate need and God's abundant provision.

The Sacrifices

In the sacrificial system that God gave through Moses, five different sacrifices were required: the sin offering, the trespass offering, the burnt offering, the meal offering and the peace offering. When viewed all together, these five reveal the significance and the blessings that were to come to New Testament believers through Christ's one complete sacrifice on the cross; no one type of sacrifice was capable of portraying all of Christ's perfect, final work on Calvary.

In this chapter we will study two of the five sacrifices: the sin and trespass offerings. In the next chapter we will discuss the three remaining offerings.

The blood of thousands of animal sacrifices...served as a graphic reminder of sin's seriousness, man's desperate need and God's abundant provision.

The Sin Offering

The compulsory sin offering, the most important of all sacrifices, was necessary because God judges what we *are* as well as what we *do*. He sees the *root* of our sin, our evil nature, as well as the *fruit* of our sin, our actions. The sin offering made atonement for the person of the offender instead of his offense and symbolized general redemption, not just ransom for a specific wrong, though forgiveness for such sin was included.

The sin offering atoned for an offender whose sins sprang from human weakness, lack of knowledge, insufficient consideration, hurry or carelessness (Lev. 5:1,4,15; Num. 35:11,15, 22). It was required when the harm done by a person's sin could not be measured or undone.

Such sin offended God, but it also resulted in a deep-seated uneasiness inside the individual. This feeling of guilt and uneasiness presented barriers to the person's worship, communion with God and testimony before others, for the human heart must be at rest before God before it can worship Him in spirit and in truth or overflow with love and concern for the welfare of others. A heart plagued with fear or guilt cannot be a worshipping heart or a witnessing heart.

Although the sin offering atoned for a person who sinned unintentionally, it did not make atonement for haughty, defiant rebellion against God and His commandments. The person who committed such presumptuous sin, willfully despising and rejecting the word of God, was to be cut off from among God's people; the atonement made for them was not to include him (Num. 15:30-31).

Although the Jew knew nothing about a sin offering for sins of presumption, there *is* such a sin offering for us. Even our presumptuous sins were laid on Jesus: our willful sins, our sins against revealed truth, are pardoned by His blood.

Mercy is sometimes regarded as a right rather than a free, unmerited gift of grace. Ignorance is often treated as if it were synonymous with guiltlessness, but *no* sin—even a sin of ignorance—can be atoned for without the shedding of blood.

We who are so prone to condone and ignore our wrongdoings should stop and ask ourselves this question: If a sin of ignorance renders me guilty before God, what must a deliberate, willful sin do? Only then can we begin to comprehend the dreadful necessity for our suffering Savior and His bloody cross. What a law by which mankind is bound! How severe. How searching. How holy and how pure our God must be!

Because of God's purity and holiness, because of mankind's deep-felt need for forgiveness and freedom from guilt, God's way of delivering those who sinned could not be by denying their sin and passing over it, but by providing and accepting an atonement for it. The sin offering represented humanity's desperate need for which a gracious, merciful God had made marvelous provision.

A Picture of Sin's Severity

The sin offering served as a vivid portrayal of the severity of sin and its consequences. To restore communion with God when it had been broken through sin, the offerer brought his

---

*The sin offering made atonement
for the person of the offender
instead of his offense and
symbolized general redemption.*

---

sacrificial animal to the priest. To demonstrate that this animal was to be a personal substitute for the offender, the sacrificer laid hands on the animal's head with the full force of the offender's weight, as if laying the whole weight of sin upon the substitute and thus transmitting personal guilt to the sacrifice.

As the offerer laid hands upon the animal, the offender confessed the specific sin and repeated a prayer of repentance, asking God to let this sacrifice serve as an atonement, or covering, for the sin. Then, taking full responsibility for the victim's death, the offerer slew the animal. If the sinner was a ruler or a commoner, the priest poured the blood on the brazen altar and burned all the fat as a sacrifice.

When the offering was completed, the priest took a portion of the meat and ate it in the court of the tabernacle. This act symbolized that the people's sin passed into the very substance of the priest, and by eating this meat he became a type of Him who was "made sin for us" (2 Cor. 5:21).

The procedure, however, differed for a sin offering made on behalf of a priest or an entire congregation. In that case a priest took some of the blood of the sacrifice into the holy place of the tabernacle. There he sprinkled it outside the veil behind which the Lord dwelt, thus symbolizing that our communion with God is by blood, and then upon the altar on which incense burned, showing that the power of prevailing intercession lies in the blood; the sinner's prayers had been heard.

The priest then went back out to the court where he poured the remainder of the blood upon the altar of sacrifice, signifying atonement. He burned all the animal's fat upon the altar, but what remained of the bull—the hide, carcass and meat—was carried outside the camp and burned (Lev. 4:11-12). Having come to represent sin, it had to be totally destroyed.

Responsibility and Accountability of Priests

New Testament believers may be surprised when they read the fourth chapter of Leviticus carefully. The type of animal brought for the sin offering depended upon the position of the person offering it.

For example, a ruler was required to offer a male goat. An individual representing no authority offered a female goat. A bullock, however, was required for the personal sins of a priest, and a bullock was also required for the sin of an entire congregation. This implies that God considered the sin of a spiritual leader to be equal to the sin of a whole congregation. Why?

Once again we see underscored the seriousness and severity of sin. A religious leader, anointed and placed in that position of authority to represent God and to teach God's ways, could lead an entire congregation, an entire nation, into sin by his example and mode of life.

As the old saying goes, "The teacher who sins teaches sin." The higher one's position, prominence and enlightenment, the greater the sin, for a leader is like the town clock by which citizens set their watches. It's clear to see why a person in a place of authority was—and is—accountable and responsible to God for his or her example and influence.

---

*While the sin offering atoned
for the sinful nature of the offender,
the trespass offering atoned
for one specific offense.*

The Trespass Offering

The sin offering and the trespass offering were alike in that both were compulsory and both were made to restore broken fellowship with God. But while the sin offering (*hatta'th*) related to the root of a person's sinful condition, his or her *evil nature*, the trespass offering (*'asham*) dealt with the fruit of that evil nature: *evil action*. Or, to explain it another way, while the sin offering atoned for the *sinful nature* of the offender, the trespass offering atoned for *one specific offense*.

When certain rights of God or men were violated, the wrong had to be righted, the broken law honored and the sin atoned for by a trespass, or guilt, offering. God enumerated several specific sins for which a trespass offering was required.

In a day when the church seems to place more emphasis on forgiveness than on obedience, believers must understand that God does not close His eyes to the "little" things we sometimes treat so carelessly. We can all benefit by carefully studying the list of sins for which God required a trespass offering:
- withholding truth (Lev. 5:1);
- contamination of the body (or spirit) through touching the unclean (Lev. 5:2-3);
- breaking vows, promises or contracts (Lev. 5:4);
- dishonesty against God or man (Lev. 5:15-16);
- sins committed due to ignorance of God's Word or failure

67

to discover and obey His will (Lev. 5:17);
- irresponsibility with another's possessions (Lev. 6:2);
- unjustness in a partnership or relationship (Lev. 6:2);
- unwarranted exertion of force or power in regard to another's rights or possessions (Lev. 6:2);
- obtaining by deception (Lev. 6:2);
- failing to return lost articles (Lev. 6:2-3).

How's that for a thought-provoking list? How often have we casually excused such sins in ourselves?

The Principle of Restitution

The most notable difference between the sin offering and the trespass offering was this: The trespass offering required that restitution be made to the person wronged and a fine be paid to the priest equal to one-fifth of the value of the restitution. The animal sacrifice (made similarly to the sin offering) made atonement to *God*, while restitution made compensation to the *victim*.

Furthermore, when a person was wronged, the restitution had to be made *before* the trespass offering was brought to the priest. The offender had to make amends with the person offended before seeking pardon from God. In other words, in the case of defrauding *God*, the proper order was first sacrifice, then restitution; in the case of defrauding a *person*, it was first restitution, then sacrifice.

The principle of restitution has not been abolished. Jesus Himself reinforced this practical truth:

> Therefore if you bring your gift to the altar, and there remember that your brother has something against you, leave your gift there before the altar, and go your

---

*In the case of defrauding God, the proper
order was first sacrifice, then restitution;
in the case of defrauding a person,
it was first restitution, then sacrifice.*

---

way. First be reconciled to your brother, and then
come and offer your gift (Matt. 5:23-24).

Approaching God with an unrighted wrong against a neighbor will not bring acceptance. But when we go to the person and right the wrong, we can claim God's gracious promise of forgiveness (Eph. 4:32; Col. 3:13).

The trespass offering required a visible expression of guilt, humiliation and confession as well as restitution. The guilty party was required to make confession "in that thing" (Lev. 5:5). This was not repeating some vague ritual or liturgical formula; it was confession of the specific sin committed. It was understood that these offerings atoned for sin only when accompanied by real repentance.

What thought-provoking symbolism. Offering a costly sacrifice. Publicly confessing sin. Laying on hands and transferring guilt. Slaying an innocent victim and watching it suffer and shed its blood for one's own wrongdoing. In these ways the seriousness of sin and the awesome holiness of God were visibly, tangibly expressed to the Jewish people.

Just think, if we were to put God's principle of restitution back into our own legal system, the whole criminal justice system could be turned around. But, as we have seen, restitution doesn't apply only to hardened criminals; the principle also applies in the church as we Christians deal with one another.

One of the major causes for the hypocrisy, judging, bitterness and lack of unity in churches today is our ignorance of God's principle of restitution and our failure to practice it.

When we Christians neglect this important principle, we bring shame upon the name of the Lord and provoke disillusionment and disappointment in one another. As New Testament priests we must keep our commitments, honor our contracts, pay our debts, make restitution for wrongs and demonstrate true repentance for our sins.

But what is true repentance? Some people equate repentance with weeping at the altar or with being sorry that they "got caught" in their sin. But the three Greek words for repentance used in the New Testament don't convey any such ideas. The first, *metanoeo*, means a change of *mind* (Matt. 3:1; Mark 1:15). The second, *metanolomai*, means a change of *heart* (Matt. 21:29,32; Heb. 7:21). The third, *metanoia*, means a change of *course*, or *life*. All three must go together for genuine repentance. All three indicate a change. Unless there is a change, there has been no repentance.

The Day of Atonement

Yet even with the deepest repentance and the most scrupulous observance of the sin offering by Israel and her priests, many sins and defilements would still remain unacknowledged, and therefore without cleansing. This need was met by the day of atonement, a day appointed for a yearly, general and perfect atonement for all the sins and uncleanness which had remained unatoned for and uncleansed.

The day of atonement was the most solemn day of the year for Israel, for on this day, by special sacrifice, an entire year's sins were covered and the nation was reconciled to her God

---

*The day of atonement was the most solemn
day of the year for Israel...by special
sacrifice, an entire year's sins were covered
and the nation was reconciled to her God.*

(see Lev. 16; 23:26-32; Num. 29:7-11).

Yet the atonement, being only a temporary provision, was
incapable of removing sin. As Hebrews 10:3-4 reveals, the
atonement had to be performed every year until Christ Himself
came to die as the Lamb of God whose blood would take
away—not simply temporarily cover—the sin of the world and
leave mankind justified: "But in those sacrifices there is a
reminder of sins every year. For it is not possible that the blood
of bulls and goats could take away sins."

On this one day of the year, as a picture of the redemption
Christ would bring, the high priest offered the atoning sacrifices. First he laid aside all his glorious garments—the breast-
plate and the robe of the ephod fringed with pomegranates and
tinkling bells, the curious girdle and golden crown. In place of
those beautiful garments, the high priest put on plain white linen
vestments similar to those worn by ordinary priests.

On this day the high priest offered fifteen sacrificial victims
in all: the morning sacrifice; the sacrifices for the high priest,
the priesthood and the people; the festive burnt offerings of the
priests and the people along with another sin offering; and, last
of all, the evening sacrifice (Heb. 9:7, 11 12).

On that day only, the high priest entered four times into the
holy of holies (spoken of as "once" in Hebrews 9:7). Every
eye was focused upon the sanctuary as the figure of the
white-robed high priest slowly disappeared within the holy

place and then out of sight behind the veil of the holy of holies.

Since the heavy, beautifully embroidered veil separated the outer sanctuary of the holy place from the holy of holies, the awesome scene I am about to describe for you was never viewed by anyone except the high priest himself.

The lid of the ark, the mercy seat, was covered with solid gold. On each end, standing upright and facing the other, a golden figure of a cherubim looked down upon the mercy seat; the wings of the figures stretched forward toward the center of the lid. The tablets of the Law along with a pot of manna and Aaron's rod were also inside the ark (Ex. 25:16,22; Heb. 9:4).

All of this was very impressive and beautiful, but when the high priest entered the holy shrine, it was the sight of the dazzling, dreadful *shechinah* cloud, God's holy presence brooding over the mercy seat between the cherubim, that caused his heart to pound and his knees to tremble.

Separated from all the people, the high priest stood alone with the red coals in his censer glowing in the darkness of the holy of holies. Can you imagine his speechless awe as he stood before that shimmering cloud, the visible presence of God, fully aware that if his own sin were not covered, if his service was not accepted, he would be a dead man?

The high priest entered the holy of holies the first time to offer incense. Sifting the incense through his fingers, onto the glowing coals in the censer, he waited for billows of fragrant smoke to fill the most holy place. At last the high priest emerged from the sanctuary, and the people knew God had accepted his service.

The high priest entered the holy of holies three more times. First he carried the blood of the bullock and sprinkled it upon the mercy seat, taking care that the sin-laden blood never spotted his white garments. Next he entered to sprinkle the

---

When the atonement was finally completed, the high priest...lifted his hands in blessing over them and cried: "You are clean from all your sins!"

---

blood of a goat. Last of all he entered to remove the censer and incense dish he had left there.

Through these sacrifices and sprinklings of blood the high priest cleansed the sanctuary, obtained forgiveness of sins and restored and secured the Old Testament privileges of sacrifices and consequential access to God.

When the atonement was finally completed, the high priest came out of the tabernacle to the great crowd of people waiting outside. He lifted his hands in blessing over them and cried: "You are clean from all your sins!"

At the end of the solemn ceremonies the high priest removed the linen garments he had worn, and they were hidden away, never to be used again.

Jesus, Our Atonement

In the same way that the high priest exchanged his gorgeous garments for humble white linen, our great High Priest, the Lord Jesus Christ, laid aside His glory with the Father and put on the plain robe of humanity when He came to make atonement for us. Paul wrote that Jesus

stripped Himself [of all privileges and rightful dignity] so as to assume the guise of a servant (slave), in that He became like men and was born a human being.

73

And after He had appeared in human form He abased and humbled Himself [still further] and carried His obedience to the extreme of death, even the death of [the] cross (Phil. 2:7-8, Amplified).

Here Paul pictured Jesus as both the officiating High Priest and as the sacrifice for sin. He was both the victim and the High Priest officiating in offering that victim. He was the Lamb without blemish, and He was also the Priest who laid the sacrifice upon the fire and sprinkled its blood upon the altar. The writer of Hebrews says simply: "He offered up Himself" (Heb. 7:27).

The Word of God also pictures Jesus as the trespass offering for New Testament believers, for He bore our guilt and humiliation and made restitution to God for our sins against Him. In the prophetic words of Isaiah, "He was wounded for our transgressions" (Is. 53:5). Paul explained how the wonderful work of forgiveness was accomplished:

And you, being dead in your trespasses...He has made alive together with Him, having forgiven you all trespasses, having wiped out the handwriting of requirements that was against us, which was contrary to us. And He has taken it out of the way, having nailed it to the cross (Col. 2:13-14).

When there was no way we could pay the penalty for our wrongdoing, Jesus Christ paid a debt He did not owe and made atonement for us. He became our sin and trespass offering.

As Jesus suffered on the cross, the sun's light unexplainably faded. By three o'clock in the afternoon, darkness enveloped the land. It was just about the time when the evening sacrifice

---

*If the Levites were obligated
to offer up sacrifices
under the old order, how much more
do we as New Testament priests.*

---

would have been offered; the priest would have been standing before the veil in the holy place offering incense. Just then, across the city, Jesus cried, "Father, into Your hands I commit My spirit," and died. At that moment the heavy veil of the holy of holies was torn in two from top to bottom, and an earthquake shook the ground (Matt. 27:45-51; Luke 23:45-46; Mark 15:33-38).

Because Jesus, God's perfect Lamb, shed His blood, the forbidding veil has been rent from top to bottom, opening the way into God's presence. Just think of it. The veil that for centuries excluded all but the high priest from God's holy presence is open today. You and I can walk right into the throne room. We can bring our praises and needs directly to God.

We are instructed in the Scriptures not to neglect so great a salvation. Serving as a priest to the most high God is not something one does every now and then when he or she has a little spare time. We have not been given such privilege without responsibility. If the Levites were obligated to offer up sacrifices under the old order, how much more do we as New Testament priests—we who have the privilege of going within the veil—bear the responsibility of offering daily sacrifices of praise and prayers of intercession as incense before God.

SEVEN

AT PEACE
WITH GOD

Come, Benjamin," called Zadok from the tent door to his young son restlessly wandering about a neighboring campfire. "Come, sit here beside me, and let's talk while your mother gets the baby ready for bed."

Zadok spread a blanket on the ground damp with the evening dew, sat down and beckoned his son to join him. When the boy was settled, Zadok asked, "Is something troubling you, Benjamin?"

The boy looked away for a moment, then answered, "Yes, Father. There's something I've been wanting to ask you, something I don't understand. Every day, morning and evening, the priests sacrifice a lamb on the altar in the courtyard outside the tabernacle. I've watched for weeks now, and it's always the same.

"And the fire on the altar, Father," the boy continued, deep in thought. "The fire never goes out. Each evening just before I drift off to sleep, I see its flickering rays glowing softly through the door of our tent."

Zadok sat quietly, enjoying the stillness of the twilight, waiting for his son's troubled questions to surface like tiny bubbles in a pot of water beginning to boil.

"Why do the lambs have to die, dawn after dawn, sunset after sunset, Father?" the boy asked after a long pause. "Why the fire?"

Long moments passed as Zadok searched his heart for simple words to describe the deep-settled beliefs by which he lived and ordered his actions. Then he spoke. "Benjamin," he said, stroking his thick, black beard, "our God's everlasting justice, flaming forth against all evil and wrongdoing, is declared to Israel in the fire on the altar. Our whole camp sees this fire burning in the open court, feeding on the sacrifice all night long, and the flames speak to us."

"The flames *speak* to you? What do they say, Father?" asked the boy breathlessly.

"As the hungry fire swallows victim after victim, day after day, it warns, 'So shall you perish unless you repent!' " replied Zadok. "But the crackling of the flames also whispers to us that there is a way of escape. The fire tells us that the sufferings

---

Some day a perfect victim shall be laid on His altar whose blood shall quench in mercy the flames that heaven kindled in judgment.

---

of its victims are seen night and day by our holy, loving God and accepted in our stead.

"You see, Benjamin," Zadok continued, "the fire is a token of our God's pledge to us that some day a perfect victim shall be laid on His altar whose blood shall quench in mercy the flames that heaven kindled in judgment. But even then the fire of our love for Him shall never die out upon the hidden altars of our hearts, for love begets love. We shall always love the God who first loved us and whose mercy kept the hungry flames at bay until the perfect sacrifice could be found."

Zadok paused to let the awesome truths sink in, then spoke once more. "You need not fear the fire nor the sacrifices, my son," he said softly. "We men of Israel who understand the language of the fire go to sleep each night and rest in peace. Benjamin, from this night forth, whenever you open your eyes in the darkness and see the fire's flickering rays glowing through the door of our tent, remember that the fire is speaking to you of our holy God's *mercy* and *love*, and be comforted."

Jesus Christ's perfect sacrifice of Himself, His shed blood on Calvary, satisfied the demands of God's holiness, made provision for mankind's forgiveness and established our peace with God. Therefore, you and I no longer have to offer the blood of lambs, bulls or goats as a substitute for our sins and shortcomings. Neither must we work or strive to obtain our salvation. The tears and labors of an entire lifetime cannot purchase our redemption, but, thank God, they do not have to. *Jesus paid it all.*

The sin offering and trespass offering spoke of mankind's need for cleansing, reconciliation and restoration to fellowship with God. Once the sin problem was under the blood, the remaining sacrifices took on a new emphasis.

The three Old Testament sacrifices we describe in this chapter express right relationship with God and fellowship with Him. They were rituals of consecration, dedication and thanksgiving, and they celebrated the covenant relationship God's people enjoyed with Him. In these sacrifices, holiness and joy joined hands.

The Burnt Offering

The burnt offering, described in Leviticus 6:8-13, was offered every day, morning and evening. On ordinary days a yearling lamb was sacrificed; on the Sabbath, two lambs were offered morning and evening (Num. 28:9-10). Because of the regularity and frequency with which this sacrifice was offered, it was called the "continual" burnt offering (Ex. 29:42).

In addition to the public burnt offerings, Israelites could also offer private burnt offerings, and this was the normal sacrifice of a Jew in proper covenant relationship with God.

The burnt offering represented self-devotion and the seeking of divine favor. The sacrifice was entirely voluntary (Lev. 1:3), as all our gifts to God must be if they are to be pleasing and acceptable to Him.

The offerer laid his hands upon the animal that was about to die, recognizing that it was to become a personal substitute. Then the offerer, being the person for whom it was to die, slew the animal. Next the priests, Aaron's sons, sprinkled the

---

*Once the sin problem was under the blood,
the remaining sacrifices took
on a new emphasis...right relationship
with God and fellowship with Him.*

---

animal's blood upon the altar and prepared the offering for sacrifice.

Since the entire animal, except the blood, was reduced to ashes and smoke, the offering symbolized the complete consecration of the self, the irrevocable giving of one's entire being to the will and purposes of God. The writer of Hebrews tells us that the burnt offering pictures Christ's voluntary sacrifice of His own body for our sanctification: "We have been made holy (consecrated and sanctified) through the offering made once for all of the body of Jesus Christ, the Anointed One" (Heb. 10:10, Amplified).

New covenant priests are also commanded to make spiritual sacrifices. The apostle Peter commanded believers, God's dedicated priesthood, to offer up those spiritual sacrifices that are acceptable and well-pleasing to God through Jesus Christ (1 Pet. 2:5) and to give Him the glory due His name.

Just as Old Testament priests offered daily burnt offerings to the Lord, we New Testament priests should daily present ourselves—our complete persons, all our members and faculties—to God. In Paul's words:

> I beseech you therefore, brethren, by the mercies of God, that you present your bodies *a living sacrifice,* holy, acceptable to God, which is your reasonable service (Rom. 12:1, italics mine).

After giving *ourselves* to God, we can give Him our *service*.
God wants us to offer our faith as well, even if it means laying down our lives for the sake of the gospel. Hebrews 11:6 says, "Without faith it is impossible to please Him." Paul, too, spoke of an offering of faith in these words addressed to the believers at Philippi:

> Holding fast the word of life, so that I may rejoice in the day of Christ that I have not run in vain or labored in vain. Yes, and if I am being poured out *as a drink offering* on the sacrifice and service of your faith, I am glad and rejoice with you all. For the same reason you also be glad and rejoice with me (Phil. 2:16-18).

Anticipating the nearness of his death, the great-hearted apostle was implying his willingness, if necessary, to be martyred for the sake of these beloved believers. To explain his devotion, he used the striking analogy of a priest slain while faithfully performing his duties. Paul pictured himself as a ministering priest offering the Philippians' faith up to God as he himself is slain. The priest's life-blood was poured out upon the sacrifice of their faith, just as the Jews poured a wine offering at the side of the altar or heathens of the day poured wine upon their sacrificial victims.

The aged apostle went on to explain to the Philippians that the mingling of their faith and his blood together on the altar, a mutual sacrifice, would mean their mutual joy.

In the midst of fiery trials and the flames of severe testing, do we ever stop to think that we are offering our faith, however weak it may seem, as a sacrifice upon the altar of God? Do we, like Job, look up at God and vow: "Though He slay me, yet will I trust Him" (Job 13:15)?

In the midst of fiery trials and the flames of severe testing, do we ever stop to think that we are offering our faith... as a sacrifice upon the altar of God?

In these days of growing persecution, has it dawned upon comfortable churchgoers that some of us may join the innumerable, ever-growing company of believers from other nations who have already been called upon to give their lives for the cause of Christ? Should that day ever dawn for you or for me, may we, like Paul, stand ready to offer our lives with joy.

The Meal Offering

The meal offering was voluntary and represented the first-fruits of the worshipper's labors. This offering was the only one of the five sacrifices in which animal flesh was not used. Here the ingredients were uncooked flour, roasted grain and unleavened cakes (Lev. 2:1-16; 6:14-18). The priest took a handful of the meal offering, put it on a vessel, laid frankincense on it, salted it, then placed it on the fire. The rest of the offering belonged to the priests.

This offering, symbolizing fellowship and communion with God, reminded the people that God gave them their food and sustenance and that they, in turn, owed Him their lives and their service as a gift.

New-covenant priests no longer sacrifice a literal meal offering to God. Instead, our generosity, kindness and good deeds are pleasing sacrifices. As the author of Hebrews commanded: "But to do good and to communicate forget not: for with such *sacrifices* God is well pleased" (Heb. 13:16, KJV, italics mine).

We all know what it means to "do good," but what does it mean "to communicate"? The word used here, surprisingly enough, is *koinonia*, meaning "to fellowship, commune, share in common." Verse 16 could be translated, "Be not forgetful of good deeds and of *fellowship*."

Can you believe what the author of Hebrews is teaching? Giving of ourselves in fellowship, communing with one another, doing good deeds—these are all sacrifices by which we please God. Almost weekly I learn of Christians who are offering such sacrifices.

For example, one evening a husband and wife, members of one of our home cell groups, were notified that their three sons had been in a terrible car wreck and taken by ambulance to a Dallas hospital.

When two of the church elders rushed to the hospital, they found five cell-group leaders and their wives already there in the waiting room, interceding for the three young men, all in critical condition and near death. Inside the intensive care unit the parents—graced with a calmness and peace from God— were moving from the bedside of one son to the bedside of another. As the elders' prayers joined the intercession already rising on behalf of those boys and their parents, God heard and answered. All three sons recovered completely.

People seem to find opportunities for ministry everywhere. One couple operates a home for battered or homeless women who have no other place to which they can turn for shelter and counsel. A healthy widow in her seventies volunteers several hours each week to minister to homebound adults. She runs errands for her shut-in friends and contacts them frequently by phone to make sure they are all right.

As the author of Hebrews commanded: "But to do good and to communicate forget not: for with such sacrifices God is well pleased."

A woman whose profession is particularly demanding keeps a supply of beautiful cards on hand. When she hears that a friend or acquaintance is ill, discouraged or going through a difficult time, she mails a card and keeps that person in her prayers.

One couple whose elderly, failing mothers live in other states sends money each month so one mother can get her hair done and the other can pay for help with the housework.

These Christians and others like them are not ministering only to people in need; they are ministering to God. Our spiritual sacrifices of fellowship, compassion and selfless devotion do not go unnoticed by the Lord. We experience the joy and satisfaction of helping others now. But some day God Himself will thank us personally:

> Then the King will say to those on His right hand, "Come, you blessed of My Father, inherit the kingdom prepared for you from the foundation of the world: for I was hungry and you gave Me food; I was thirsty and you gave Me drink; I was a stranger and you took Me in; I was naked and you clothed Me; I was sick and you visited Me; I was in prison and you came to Me." Then the righteous will answer Him, saying, "Lord, when did we see You hungry and feed You, or thirsty and give You drink?" And the King

will answer and say to them, "Assuredly, I say to you, inasmuch as you did it to one of the least of these My brethren, you did it to Me" (Matt. 25:34-37,40).

James, known as the brother of our Lord, reduced true religion to a very simple formula: "Pure and undefiled religion before God and the Father is this: to visit orphans and widows in their trouble, and to keep oneself unspotted from the world" (James 1:27).

Jesus Himself said the same thing to the self-righteous Pharisees. He sternly commanded, "Go and learn what this means: 'I desire mercy and not sacrifice' " (Matt. 9:13). This means that God longs to see our hearts and hands extended to the needy. His great heart cries for the day when we will take time to visit the sick, lonely and distressed and bless them with the gifts of our presence, encouragement and prayers. It means that our obedience and wholehearted adherence to the gentle laws of love and mercy are much more desirable to God than the fat of rams (1 Sam. 15:22). It means that if we will not offer Him the costly sacrifices of pure lives and compassionate hearts, then He's not interested in carnal substitutes, no matter how deeply we dig into our wallets for some charitable donation.

When it comes to being conformed to the image of Christ, the bottom line is not attending church, tithing, witnessing, singing in the choir and memorizing Scripture. The bottom line is love. Jesus Christ says, "If you want to be like Me, you must feel and demonstrate compassion." The new-covenant priest has no other option.

One meaning of the meal offerings is similar to that of the offering of the tithes; it is expressed in the words of David:

In his letter to the Philippian believers who had contributed to his needs, Paul called their gifts "a sweet-smelling aroma, an acceptable sacrifice, well pleasing to God."

All that is in heaven and in earth is Yours....
All things come from You,
And of Your own we have given You (1 Chr. 29:11,14).

God is well-pleased with our sacrifices of good deeds and fellowship, but He has also commanded us as New Testament priests to offer our gifts and offerings. The root word of the Old Testament word translated as *offering* means "to draw near." When we think of an *offering* as that by which we draw near to God, giving becomes a privilege and a delight, not an unpleasant obligation.

In his letter to the Philippian believers who had contributed to his needs, Paul called their gifts "a sweet-smelling aroma, an acceptable *sacrifice,* well pleasing to God" (Phil. 4:18, italics mine). When we give so that the work of the Lord may progress and God's laborers be supplied, we have the joy of knowing that our gifts and offerings are acceptable to God Himself.

Like the Jewish worshippers of long ago, we New Testament believers should first give ourselves to God. After we give Him ourselves, then He will anoint and accept our service and gifts, the firstfruits of our labors. The order cannot be reversed. Good works and dollar bills will never be accepted by God as substitutes for our obedient, devoted hearts.

The Peace Offering

Of the five Old Testament sacrifices, the peace offering was the most joyous. Called a "peace offering" because it was offered by those who were at peace with God, it expressed gratitude and obligation to God; it was an opportunity to fellowship with Him.

Of all the sacrifices, the peace offering was to be observed last. Perhaps this was to underscore the fact that peace comes as a result of obeying God and meeting His requirements.

The peace offerings could be either public or private. The two lambs offered every year at Pentecost were a public peace offering, regarded as most holy. Their flesh was eaten within the holy place by the officiating priests. Public peace offerings were also offered on occasions of great corporate rejoicing or solemnity.

Private peace offerings were of three kinds: sacrifices of thanksgiving offered in acknowledgment of mercies received (Lev. 7:12), vows (Lev. 7:16) and voluntary offerings given from loving hearts (Lev. 7:16). These sacrifices were always accompanied by a drink offering and a meal offering consisting of coarsely ground grain and fine flour mixed with oil or unleavened cakes prepared in three different ways with oil (Lev. 7:11-14).

The offerer was required to lay hands upon the sacrifice, make confession and give thanks to God. After the offerer slew the sacrifice, the priest sprinkled the blood upon the altar and then offered the fat and innards to the Lord. The peace offering ended in a joyous feast on the sacrificed animal's meat and the cakes.

The offerer, his friends and the priests joined in happy fellowship with their God in the court of the tabernacle (Deut.

---

*Called a "peace offering" because
it was offered by those who were
at peace with God...it was an
opportunity to fellowship with Him.*

12:17-18). This meal denoted the fellowship between the worshipper and God; it symbolized and pledged friendship and peace with Him.

In the old-covenant peace offering, the Jews offered thanksgiving along with their sacrifices. Thankful praise is also a type of sacrifice that the new-covenant priest is to offer.

> Through Him therefore let us constantly and at all times offer up to God *a sacrifice of praise*, which is the fruit of lips that thankfully acknowledge and confess and glorify His name (Heb. 13:15, Amplified, italics mine).

Did you notice that the writer commands us to offer the sacrifice of praise *continually*—not simply, as the Jews did, on certain occasions, but always? And in our praise we are also instructed to confess His name thankfully. Christ teaches us to praise God's name in the first phrase of the Lord's prayer: "Our Father which art in heaven, Hallowed be Thy name." As we do this, we confess who God is and what He has done for us.

But praise to God for who He is and for His marvelous works is not the only sacrifice of praise that God accepts. God's Word teaches that He regards the confession of our sins as a form of praise offering. God, who creates the fruit of the lips (Is. 57:19), tells us exactly what to do when we stumble and fall due to our iniquity:

> Take with you words, and return to the Lord. Say to Him, Take away all our iniquity, accept what is good and receive us graciously: so will we render our thanks as bullocks [to be sacrificed] and pay the confession of our lips (Hos. 14:2, Amplified).

The psalmist also wrote of the sacrifice of repentance:

> "My sacrifice (the sacrifice acceptable) to God is a broken spirit; a broken and a contrite heart—broken down with sorrow for sin and humbly and thoroughly penitent—such, O God, You will not despise (Ps. 51:17, Amplified).

We priests should never allow a sense of guilt or failure to drive us away from God's presence. Instead, when we sin, we should take our broken spirits and contrite hearts to God and offer Him a sacrifice of thanksgiving for His great mercy and forgiveness. He will receive us gladly.

Another offering of praise that pleases the Lord is songs and joyful shouts of praise to God even in the presence of our enemies and in the midst of trials. Like the psalmist, we should declare:

> And now shall my head be lifted up above my enemies round about me; in His tent I will offer sacrifices and shouting of joy; I will sing, yes, I will sing praises to the Lord (Ps. 27:6, Amplified, italics mine).

The instruction Paul gave to the Colossians is good advice

When we sin, we should take our broken spirits and contrite hearts to God and offer Him a sacrifice of thanksgiving for His great mercy and forgiveness.

---

for modern-day believers:

> Let the word of Christ dwell in you richly in all wisdom, teaching and admonishing one another in psalms and hymns and spiritual songs, singing with grace in your hearts to the Lord. And whatever you do in word or deed, do all in the name of the Lord Jesus, giving thanks to God the Father through Him (Col. 3:16-17).

As we go about our day-to-day business, let us learn to offer up continual spiritual sacrifices of praise and thanksgiving.

The peace offering is the point toward which the other sacrifices lead us: Once we have been brought near to God through Christ's sacrificial merit, not only is there no condemnation, but access to grace is assured, and joy is ours.

Just as Old Testament priests and believers were to partake of the peace offering joyously, new-covenant believers who gather at the Lord's table to observe communion are to feast together upon His abundant provision and thankfully recall how Jesus suffered and died for them. "The cup of blessing which we bless, is it not the communion of the blood of Christ? The bread which we break, is it not the communion of the body of Christ?" (1 Cor. 10:16).

The peace offering symbolizes the wonderful promise expressed in Revelation 3:20: "Behold, I stand at the door and knock. If anyone hears My voice and opens the door, I will come in to him and dine with him, and he with Me." Joyous celebration and intimate communion await us. All we have to do is open the door.

Lessons for Today

Impressive ceremonies, gorgeous rituals, symbolic sacrifices—all point to Jesus; all teach us more about what God requires in our service and worship today.

Has the Holy Spirit ever prompted you to bring the Lord a peace offering—a vow or voluntary offering from a loving heart, some sacrifice of thanksgiving in acknowledgment of mercies received? Perhaps you brought part of your bonus or gave a special offering from some unexpected financial blessing. Maybe your gratitude for the Lord's goodness overflowed, and you decided to skip a meal and spend the time ministering to the Lord in praise and worship. Peace offerings are wonderful, joyous occasions of friendship and fellowship with God.

But sometimes God asks us to do something that makes us miserable before it makes us happy. If you've ever experienced one of those times of testing and stretching, you have an idea of how I felt when God asked me to give Him my son.

It was 1977. I was still serving as youth pastor at Beverly Hills Baptist Church, and Melva and I were living in a lovely four-bedroom home in south Dallas. John Aaron, our first child, was three years old. He was a cute little blond tyke, and Melva Jo and I adored him. As a matter of fact, we were coming to the place that many young parents reach: We almost idolized our child.

But I began having a horrible, recurring dream. Three times

---

*Peace offerings are
wonderful, joyous occasions
of friendship and
fellowship with God.*

I dreamed that John Aaron had died. The first time I passed it off as just a nightmare. When I dreamed the same thing the second time, I noted it but shrugged it off. When I dreamed the third time that my son had died, I knew the Lord was trying to say something to me. I crawled out of bed and tiptoed to the guest room that doubled as my study and place of prayer. I quietly closed the door, and God and I got down to business.

As I knelt there in the darkness, the Spirit of God spoke to me in my heart and asked, "Will you give Me your son?"

By this time in my life I knew I was to be careful how I answered the Lord. I remembered the time I was preaching in India: God asked me if I'd sell everything Melva and I owned and give it to His work. I told Him yes, and He held me to our agreement. (I should tell you that after Melva and I obeyed, the Lord unexpectedly allowed us to buy and pay off the home where we were living when this incident with the dreams took place. But I knew better than to give God some flippant answer whenever He asked if I would do something.)

I knelt there in the dark that night, crying and wrestling with this soul-wrenching decision. But a few minutes later when the question came to me a second time, God gave me the grace to answer, "Yes, Lord. I'll give You my son."

I remember saying, "Lord, I dedicated John Aaron to You when he was born, and I will not take him back now. He's Yours."

HIGHEST CALLING

The moment those words came out of my mouth, I saw a vision of my little boy walking toward Jesus and crawling into His arms. Both John Aaron's and the Lord's faces were radiating with such glory and joy that all the fear of losing my only son was completely erased.

Watching the two of them, I said, "Lord, if John Aaron were to go home with You, I would never wish him back after what I've seen tonight."

The vision vanished, and the Lord spoke these words to my spirit: "Since you have given him to Me, I'll give him back to serve with you for many years."

I was sitting there, rejoicing in those wonderful words, when a little knock came at the door. The sound frightened me because it was four in the morning, and nobody else in the family was supposed to be awake. But when I opened the door, there looking up at me was little John Aaron.

"Daddy," he said, rubbing his eyes, "I had a dream."

Cuddling him in my arms, I asked, "What was your dream about?"

His answer rocked me back on my heels.

"I was in Jesus' arms," John Aaron lisped, "and we were so happy, Daddy. Jesus' face was shining, and we were so happy."

Crying like a baby, I woke up Melva and told her what had happened. We stayed up the rest of the night, praying and praising God.

That experience affirmed something I already knew: When God asks us to give Him something, it isn't because He needs it. It's because we need to give it. Do you see what I'm saying? The God of the universe doesn't need my money or my "stuff" or even my son. Diamonds and dollar bills are not heaven's currency. But if I have allowed anything to come between God and me, if I have held back and begrudged giving it to Him,

---

*When God asks us
to give Him something, it isn't
because He needs it.
It's because we need to give it.*

---

for my own sake I need to relinquish it to God. I must not allow anything or anyone to come between my soul and my Savior.

What are the sacrifices that New Testament priests are to offer to God? Close your eyes and see if you can list them with me:

- ourselves;
- our faith and, if need be, our very life-blood;
- our good deeds and fellowship;
- our gifts and offerings and our praise.

Our whole lives must be living sacrifices that we offer up to God. As Charles Spurgeon, the great British preacher, said so eloquently: "Sin is death. Labor to keep away from it. Get you to living things. Offer to God living prayers and living tears; love Him with living love; trust Him with living faith; serve Him with living obedience." What are we to offer? Everything!

We shall all stand before God someday. To believers who in this life allowed the great altar of sacrifice to be neglected, God might say something like this:

You were commanded to offer sacrifices to Me. Morning after morning, day after day, Jesus, your great High Priest, stood waiting for you at the altar of sacrifice, but you brought Him nothing to offer.

You did not present yourself to Him as a living sacrifice. You brought Him no praise or thanksgiving.

You chose to doubt and question rather than to put your faith and trust in His hands. I did not require your life's blood; I asked only for your testimony. Yet when the need for your witness arose, you turned away, ashamed to speak of Me.

You offered Jesus no service or good deeds. You refused to set apart a portion of those good things I had entrusted to you so that others might benefit and be blessed. Instead, you consumed it all yourself, then you tossed your leftovers at the nail-pierced feet of your High Priest.

Why did you neglect My altar? Why did you leave My Son standing beside it morning after morning with nothing pleasing to present to Me? He redeemed you with His own blood. Why had you nothing worthy to offer back to Him?

Why, indeed? I pray that neither you nor I ever have to answer that question. How about you? Are you holding something back? Your time? A talent? A person? A pleasure? A memory? If so, for your own sake, give it to God, no matter what it costs you. Like King David, you must declare, "I will not take what is yours for the Lord, nor offer...that which costs me nothing" (1 Chr. 21:24).

You need not fear. God will not waste your gift. He will invest it where it will reap the greatest rewards for you and for His kingdom. As you take care of those things that are dearest to Him, He will take care of those things that are dearest to you. After all, the God who so loved the world that He gave His only begotten Son understands sacrifice.

EIGHT

TENDING THE
GOLDEN LAMPSTAND

Man, what are you *on?*" exclaimed the pastor incredulously.

I had heard similar questions before. Chuckling at his puzzled expression, I replied, "What do you mean: What am I on?"

"You know what I mean," he said, determined not to be

sidetracked by my teasing. "I've seen the schedule you keep, and yet you have all this energy. And you're always on the cutting edge. How do you do it? Do you take drugs or vitamins or *what?*"

Other pastors sometimes approach the same subject, but from a different direction. "Larry," they caution, "you'd better slow down. Aren't you afraid of burnout?"

"I would be," I assure them, "if it were *my* fire."

I understand their concern. I remember far too well the exhaustion and frustration I battled in the seventies while attempting to balance a schedule that would make a juggler nervous. I was pastoring a dynamic youth group that eventually grew to one thousand members at Beverly Hills Baptist Church in Dallas; attempting to complete my master's degree at a seminary almost forty miles away; seeing three hundred to five hundred kids saved every month in concerts and crusades; trying to be a husband to my wife, Melva; and striving to love and provide for our two little children and a third that was on the way. No wonder I eventually wound up in the hospital, physically exhausted.

Much of my frustration and exhaustion stemmed from the fact that I didn't know how to say no to people. Consequently I was always running here and there. But that was nothing new. Looking back, I imagine that everyone who knew me, including my wife, thought of me as an exclamation mark on legs.

The first year we were married, Melva and I lived behind the church in a small mobile home. Not realizing how badly Melva and I needed time alone together, I'd invite two dozen or more kids at a time to our house for snacks and fellowship. Melva was so busy learning to cook, keep house and entertain company, and I was so busy ministering at the church and working on my master's degree, that we were also busy

---

I hadn't been rejecting the Lord; I had just slipped into the dangerous habit of neglecting Him.

---

neglecting each other. After a few months of that foolishness, I realized we weren't spending enough time together.

One afternoon I came strolling into the house in an amorous mood. But Melva was running around dusting and sweeping and cooking, trying to get ready for the company I had invited. For some reason she just wasn't interested in hugs and kisses right then. Well, my offended, twenty-one-year-old male ego and I decided it was time for me to put my foot down. I raised my voice and ordered, "Melva Jo, you leave all that stuff alone, and come on in here with me."

Melva burst out crying, and just about that time the Holy Spirit raised His voice. He ordered, "Son, *you* come on in here with *Me!*"

I walked into the tiny bedroom I used as a study, shut the door and sat down. The Lord said, "The reason your wife is so busy and is neglecting *you* is that *you* have been so busy and have been neglecting *Me.*"

When the Lord and I got through with our talk, I stumbled into the kitchen, took my wife in my arms and sobbed, "Oh, Melva, I'm so sorry. I'm so sorry."

I hadn't been *rejecting* the Lord; I had just slipped into the dangerous habit of *neglecting* Him. My priorities were all wrong. Time for prayer and Bible study were last on my list of "Things to do today."

Can you identify with what I'm saying? I had been consuming

myself—burning the candle at both ends. Now I was in trouble. I had no source of power to keep me going.

In a day when productivity is equated with spirituality, it's hard to keep our priorities straight. Sometimes it's hard to take the time to do the work of a priest and tend the golden lampstand in the sanctuary of our souls. But if we neglect that privilege, before we know it, the lamps will be smoking and flickering and threatening to burn out. Darkness and gloom will settle upon our spirits.

You see, there's much more to doing the work of a priest than just offering sacrifices. In addition to the five Old Testament sacrifices we've already studied, three other offerings were also regularly made by the priests in the holy place: (1) the twelve loaves of shewbread were renewed every Sabbath; (2) the golden lampstand was filled with oil every morning; (3) the incense for the altar of incense was renewed every morning and evening.

As we have already studied, the sanctuary of the Jews was divided into two chambers: the holy place and the holy of holies. The holy place contained three articles of furniture. A small, gold-covered altar of incense was centered in front of the forbidding veil screening the holy of holies. On the right side stood a small golden table on which sat twelve cakes of shewbread. On the left, directly opposite the table of shewbread, stood a seven-branched, five-feet-tall candlestick of pure gold. Its oil-fed lamps furnished the light in the holy place.

Because people of ancient times often set a clay, oil-burning lamp upon a three-legged stand and referred to it as a candlestick, some Bible translations refer to the golden lampstand as a candlestick. But the concept of candles and candlesticks is foreign to the biblical meaning, for lamps give light by means of oil, while candles (like many sincere but unwise believers)

---

*Lamps give light by means of oil,
while candles (like many sincere
but unwise believers) give
light by consuming themselves.*

---

give light by consuming themselves.

The tongs and snuff dishes of the beautiful lampstand were made of a talent (sixty to eighty pounds) of pure gold (Ex. 25:38). The elaborately wrought seven-branched lampstand was designed in a floral motif (see Ex. 25:31-40; 37:17-24; 39:37). The golden snuff dishes were used for bringing live coals from the great altar of burnt offering, and the tongs were used to pull up the wicks and to hold a glowing coal while the priest blew upon it to light the lamp.

The outer lamps could be relit from one of the other lamps, but the large central lamp, toward which all the others bent, could be relit only by a glowing coal from the altar of burnt offering.

Oil for the golden lampstand was prepared from olives that had been carefully washed before being beaten. Beating the olives, rather than crushing them in oil presses, rendered the finest quality, white-colored oil.

God gave Moses an explicit command regarding the golden lampstand. The lamps were to burn continually from evening until morning:

> Then the Lord spoke to Moses saying: "Command the children of Israel that they bring to you pure oil of pressed olives for the light, to make the lamps burn continually. Outside the veil of the Testimony, in the

tabernacle of meeting, Aaron shall be in charge of it from evening until morning before the Lord continually; it shall be a statute forever in your generations. He shall be in charge of the lamps on the pure gold lampstand before the Lord continually" (Lev. 24:1-4).

The lamps were lighted at the time of the evening sacrifice (Ex. 30:8), then extinguished, trimmed and filled with oil at the time of the morning sacrifice (Ex. 30:7; 1 Sam. 3:3). Tradition tells us that the lamps held only half a "log," a little more than a cup of oil; the oil had to be replenished daily if the lamps were to enjoy a sufficient supply.

Replenishing the Oil

In the Scriptures, oil is a symbol of the Holy Spirit. Understanding that the Spirit of God, not wine, is to be the source of strength and joy for the believer, Paul commanded:

"Do not be drunk with wine...but be filled with the Spirit" (Eph. 5:18). In the original text the idea is that believers are to "be being continually filled" with the Holy Spirit, just as the lamps in the holy place were continually being filled.

What did Paul mean when he made this command? I think I understand what Paul was getting at, because my father was a hard drinker for years before he came to know the Lord. I've been around wine and liquor enough to know that it takes more than a little sip once or twice a week to stay drunk. No, sir. A person gets drunk and stays drunk *by drinking*.

The same principle applies to you and me as believers. If we want to be filled with the Holy Spirit, we must "be being continually filled." Sitting on a pew or singing in the choir on Sunday won't keep us filled. We need a supply of fresh oil every

---

If we want to illuminate our dark work with the light of God, the golden lamps in the sanctuary of our souls must be daily refilled with a supply of fresh oil.

---

day, not just on Sundays.

This is why we must learn to put God first every day, receiving His cleansing and fresh anointing. Then all through the day we must "take little sips" of the wine of the Spirit, making melody in our hearts to the Lord, speaking to ourselves in psalms and hymns and spiritual songs and praying in the Spirit (Eph. 5:19; Jude 20).

If we want to illuminate our dark world with the light of God, the golden lamps in the sanctuary of our souls must be daily refilled with a supply of fresh oil.

That brings us to another point. Did you notice that the lampstand itself was not the light that illumined the darkness? It only held the oil that gave the light. You and I, standing in the positions of service to which God calls us, are only the lampstands, the vessels containing the oil of the Spirit. Without Jesus and the Holy Spirit, we can do nothing, for He is our light and our salvation (Ps. 27:1). He is our righteousness and sanctification, our peace and healing, our wisdom and strength.

Jesus taught that His followers are the light of the world (Matt. 5:14). We must not allow that light to burn dim, flicker or go out. We are to let our light so shine that those around us may see our good works and glorify our Father in heaven (Matt. 5:16).

More than a hundred years ago, George Müller of Bristol, England, discovered this principle of replenishing the oil.

Müller, remembered for his walk of faith and his work with thousands of orphans in the 1800s, reached the point in his personal consecration where he resolved that he would no longer spend his best hours in bed.

Even though he was recovering from a recurring illness that caused tremendous physical weakness, Müller determined to rise every morning at four instead of sleeping until six or seven.

His newly acquired habit of rising early secured long seasons of uninterrupted time for prayer and meditation on the Scriptures. To his surprise, Müller grew stronger physically instead of becoming weaker, and he was so overjoyed with the new physical and spiritual vigor gained from waiting upon God while others slept that he continued the habit for the remainder of his life. As a result he read the Bible from cover to cover nearly two hundred times and by faith financed a remarkable ministry with orphans.

Not too long ago a pastor with whom I am acquainted was pleasantly surprised to discover that such miraculous experiences are not reserved only for revered saints like George Müller.

Determined to see spiritual and numerical growth in his church, the pastor started setting aside two to three hours each day for intercession and communion with God. But he was dismayed when he discovered that his elderly mother, a petite, fragile woman whose health had never been good, was rising at 4:30 A.M.; she felt led by God to spend two hours a day in prayer for her children, several of whom were in the ministry.

"God," he wept one morning in frustration, "why did You ask my mother to rise so early? You know she's never been well and strong."

The concerned pastor's question was answered several weeks later when he received a letter from his mother. "Son," she

---

*As you and I do the possible, rising
early to tend the lamps and
replenish the oil of the Spirit,
God will take care of the impossible.*

---

wrote, "since I've been rising early each morning to pray for you children, my health is improving, and I feel stronger than I have in many years."

As you and I do the possible, rising early to tend the lamps and replenish the oil of the Spirit, God will take care of the impossible. He will make up that which is lacking—so that we might glorify Him. He made a special promise to those who take time to pray:

> Those who wait on the Lord shall renew their strength;
> They shall mount up with wings like eagles,
> They shall run and not be weary,
> They shall walk and not faint (Is. 40:31).

Are you battling weakness and weariness, fatigue and faintheartedness? It's time to replenish the oil.

Trimming the Lamps

The priest's ministry each morning at the golden lampstand was not completed until he carefully trimmed the lamps. He snipped away the blackened, exhausted portions of the wicks and carefully discarded them into a golden snuff dish. He covered the soot and charred fibers completely so they could not be exposed or spilled, then permanently disposed of them.

105

The act of trimming the wicks kept the light burning brightly.

If we Christians are not shining, something is in the way. We, too, must daily allow the Spirit of God to snip away the hindrances blackening our testimonies and cut off the sins threatening to quench the fire of God. We must wait in God's presence as He exchanges our charred, exhausted wicks for fresh ones. Knowing that a smoking flax He will not quench, we must trust His hand as He gently trims away the burned-out threads and fibers and blows upon our faltering flame until it leaps forth with a renewed brilliance.

Once those hindrances and sins are cut off, they are covered by the blood of Jesus and discarded from remembrance. Satan will attempt to uncover them, condemn us and call to remembrance our past failures. But we must refuse to listen to his lies. Our failures and sins have been gently removed, covered and carried away by the God who promises:

> I, even I, am He who blots out your transgressions for My own sake, and I will not remember your sins (Is. 43:25).

Each day as you and I rise from our knees with our wicks trimmed and our lamps filled with a fresh supply of oil, we don't have to worry about burnout. All we have to do is stand in our places before a sin-darkened world and let Jesus shine through us.

NINE

REPLENISHING
THE SHEWBREAD

Picture the Sabbath scene: Having risen before dawn, the priest had washed at the laver and put on his white priestly garments. The time had come to renew the twelve cakes of shewbread. As the priest entered the holy place, to his right, illuminated by the soft glow of the golden lampstand, stood the table of shewbread.

The wooden table overlaid with gold measured only two feet high, eighteen inches across and three feet in length. On the table twelve cakes of unleavened shewbread were arranged in two heaps.

The number twelve represented the twelve tribes of Israel. The cakes themselves reminded the priest of the manna with which God had miraculously fed His nation of at least two million people for more than forty years as they wandered in the barren wilderness. There God had attempted to teach a stubborn, rebellious people that their survival was as dependent upon obedience to God's words as upon the manna, meat and water so miraculously provided by His mighty hand (Deut. 8:3).

The twelve cakes of shewbread had remained in the holy place for seven days as an offering to God. Now, on the Sabbath, the priest removed the old shewbread and replaced it with twelve freshly baked cakes. Once removed from the table as an offering to God, the shewbread became provision for the needs of the priests.

The priests gathered together and partook of the shewbread each Sabbath, foreshadowing New Testament priests' gathering around the Lord's table for the breaking of bread, or communion. We also see a type of the uplifting fellowship that believers enjoy as they meet together weekly to study and feast upon the Word of God.

Feasting Upon the Living Bread

While teaching in the synagogue in Capernaum, Jesus, the Jews' long-awaited Messiah, warned His followers not to labor for food that perishes but for the enduring food He gives (John 6:27). When the Jews murmured and protested against Christ's

---

Jesus, the Jews' long-awaited Messiah, warned His followers not to labor for food that perishes but for the enduring food He gives.

---

teaching that He was the Bread of life, Jesus declared:

> Your fathers ate the manna in the wilderness, and are dead. This is the bread which comes down from heaven, that one may eat of it and not die. I am the living bread which came down from heaven. If anyone eats of this bread, he will live forever; and the bread that I shall give is My flesh, which I shall give for the life of the world.... He who feeds on Me will live because of Me (John 6:49-51,57).

Are we feeding or famishing? If our souls are hungering and thirsting after righteousness, we can be filled. If our spirits are restless, unsatisfied and unfulfilled, God invites us to His table:

> Ho! Everyone who thirsts,
> Come to the waters;
> And you who have no money,
> Come, buy and eat.
> Yes, come, buy wine and milk
> Without money and without price.
> Why do you spend money for what is not bread,
> And your wages for what does not satisfy?
> Listen diligently to Me, and eat what is good,
> And let your soul delight itself in abundance.

Incline your ear, and come to Me.
Hear, and your soul shall live (Is. 55:1-3).

Why does God issue such a magnanimous invitation? Because He made us so that our deep spiritual hunger for God is satisfied only by delighting in the glorious presence of Jesus within and feeding upon His living Word.

The true scriptural name for the shewbread is "Bread of the Face" (Ex. 25:30; 35:13; 39:36). Do you know what that name says to me? It says that you and I can rise each morning and commune with Jesus face to face and heart to heart. Like the psalmist, we can:

Seek the Lord and His strength;
Seek His face evermore (Ps. 105:4).

Knowing that His steadfast love never ceases and that His mercies are new every morning, each day we can pray, "Give us this day our daily bread." And as we feed upon His Word, as we bask in His sanctifying presence, we personally experience what to the Old Testament believer was only a beautiful benediction from an earthly high priest:

The Lord bless you and keep you;
The Lord make *His face* shine upon you,
And be gracious to you;
The Lord lift up *His countenance* upon you,
And give you peace (Num. 6:24-26, italics mine).

The Transforming Power of the Word

As I have shared in my book *Could You Not Tarry One Hour?*

The true scriptural name for the shewbread is "Bread of the Face." ...You and I can rise each morning and commune with Jesus face to face and heart to heart.

I found Jesus in 1968, when I was seventeen. My family was wealthy. I had everything, and yet I had nothing. I knew there was something missing, but I didn't know what it was. I went to church one Sunday morning, and when the preacher gave the invitation I went forward. But, sincere as he was, he didn't tell me about the blood of Jesus and the power of God. All I got was a pat on the back and a card to fill out.

Not long after that I found myself in the psychiatric ward of a nearby hospital, confused and almost completely out of touch with what was going on around me. After the doctor put me on sixteen tranquilizers a day, I spent much of the time lying flat on my back with my eyes rolled up in my head.

The day came when my brokenhearted father forced himself to tell me about a room he and the doctor were reserving for me at the state mental institution. Daddy tried to be brave and comforting as he told me how nice everything would be, but his voice shook when he explained that I'd have to get used to the walls surrounding the buildings and grounds.

My future was as dark and hopeless as a tomb. But the day before my shock treatments were to begin, for no apparent reason my mental fog seemed to lift. I lay on the floor and cried out to God for help. Over and over, one word erupted from my empty heart and echoed in my ears. It was the name of Jesus.

I didn't even know there was a verse in the Bible that promised "Whosoever shall call on the name of the Lord shall be saved"

(Acts 2:21), but Jesus knew it.

Inside my bleak, sterile hospital room, I heard His voice, and from that day to this I have feasted upon the words He spoke to me: "Now you are My son. You will be My minister and My mouth." Then, just as if He had been commanding me to take up my bed and walk, He said, "You can get up and go home."

The doctor didn't believe it. My father didn't believe it. Nobody believed it. But within four days my very puzzled doctor dismissed me from the hospital.

I preached about Jesus anywhere they would let me witness for Him. I didn't call myself to preach; I just couldn't help it. I had to tell people that Jesus was real. I knew He was, because He had talked to me. He had changed my heart and given my life meaning and purpose.

I continued to see that doctor the rest of the year because I had been on so many tranquilizers that he had to take me off them gradually. I was still reeling from the nervous breakdown But I began to live in the Word of God, and it became my meditation day and night. As God's Word also began to live in me, another miracle happened.

For as long as I could remember, reading had been a frustrating struggle for me. I had a terrible time reading aloud. I was never tested for dyslexia, but my uncle, a medical doctor, and his children are dyslexic, so I am convinced that dyslexia was my problem all through my childhood and adolescence.

I could stare at a page, but the words would not "jump" from the page to my mind. I could sound out words and syllables phonetically if I worked hard enough, but I could not force them into a sentence. I tried and tried, but after a while I just gave up. I wasn't interested in reading because it was so frustrating.

But when Jesus saved me, I began to read and study the Bible

God literally sent His Word and healed me....I've had a miracle in my mind, and I attribute that miracle primarily to reading and meditating upon the Word.

---

and to memorize Scripture. Almost immediately I noticed a startling difference: My mind and my ability to read were healed. As far as I can remember, the Bible is the first book I ever read all the way through. God literally sent His Word and healed me. Consequently, I was able to enroll in college and graduate with honors.

I've had a miracle in my mind, and I attribute that miracle primarily to reading and meditating upon the Word—to saturating my thinking with His renewing, quickening words of life.

When I wanted to go on to seminary, my doctor's approval was required because of my medical history. Not having seen me since I was a college freshman, he was amazed at hearing my achievements. He couldn't believe that the young man who had once been so devastated was now well and applying for graduate school. Finally he admitted, "I've never seen what I would consider to be a bona fide miracle before, but *you* are a miracle!"

After we talked further, he leaned forward in his chair and asked, "Would you consider going to medical school? After what you've been through, you've really got a touch to help people."

I told him I appreciated what he had said but that I was called to preach.

As I talked to him about Jesus, he confided that he was a believer—but one who had been wounded as a college student when some Christians refused to accept him because of his desire to become a psychiatrist. Our appointment ended with the two of us weeping and rejoicing together.

I was accepted at graduate school and made excellent grades all the way through the eighty-eight-hour master of divinity program. As a matter of fact, Greek was one of my favorite subjects in college and seminary. I took twenty hours of Greek and made straight A's. By graduation I could read a second language better than I had been able to read English at age seventeen.

It's a matter of nourishing one's mind daily with the bread of God's Word. The old-covenant priests received strength by partaking of the shewbread. New-covenant priests, by feasting upon the Word, partake of the Bread of life, which is able to strengthen us, heal us and sustain us physically, mentally and spiritually.

One final truth about the shewbread. Although descendants of Aaron who bore disqualifying blemishes or deformities were not permitted to minister in the holy place, they were not excluded from eating the shewbread. They could sit at the table with their fellow priests and eat their fill.

I thank God for His merciful provision for imperfect people like me. Because He didn't banish a babbling, broken, seventeen-year-old boy from His table; because He allowed me to feed upon His quickening Word and to draw strength from His healing presence, today I am ministering as His priest.

If you are imperfect, if you are blemished and weak in faith, remember: Healing is the children's bread. Run to His table daily. Feed upon the Word of God; receive the nourishment you need. And don't forget to expect *your* miracle.

TEN

INTERCEDING AT THE MERCY SEAT

It was a Saturday night in 1976, and I was exhausted after driving all the way from Dallas to the small west Texas town where I was scheduled to conduct a week-long revival. After contacting the pastor of the church where I'd be preaching, I checked into a motel, unpacked and spent some time in study and prayer. After all that I was ready for a good night's sleep.

Some time long after midnight I awoke with a start. I'd had a terrible dream that was so vivid, so real, I just couldn't shake it. I was haunted by a vision of my wife's face, wild with terror and contorted with pain as she was brutally raped then dragged through broken glass. If it were only a dream, why did it seem so real?

Gripped by a burden of intercession, I rolled out of bed, fell on my face and prayed in the Spirit with all my might. Around daybreak the voice of God spoke in my ear. "My bride here has been raped," He said. "Get up and leave this place. Don't you preach here."

Shaken but determined to obey God, I phoned the pastor who had invited me and explained what had happened. I told him I would not be preaching in his church that morning. Then I got dressed and began packing.

In less than an hour the pastor was knocking at the door of my motel room. "You're going to preach!" he insisted angrily. "I've advertised all over this town, and you *are* going to preach!"

But I would not back down. Explaining again what I had seen and repeating what God had said to me, I refused to disobey God. Instead, I got into my car and drove away.

Two weeks later when the associate pastor of that church called me, the puzzling questions in my mind were answered. "Larry," he confided, "what God showed you about the church here was exactly right. The pastor has been running around with women and stealing money from the church."

My heart went out to that congregation of abused, broken people and to their pastor, who had allowed his heart to be ruled by lust and greed. Remembering God's stern command to leave and not to preach in that place, deep in my heart I knew that

---

Around daybreak the voice of God spoke in my ear. "My bride here has been raped," He said. "Get up and leave this place. Don't you preach here."

---

the grieved Spirit of God had departed from there and had taken the cloud of God's glory with Him.

The Grieved Spirit

You see, in the days of the old covenant, when people sinned against *God the Father*, He *slew* them. In the Gospels, when people sinned in the presence of *Jesus*, He *rebuked* them. But throughout the Word of God, when people flagrantly, willfully and habitually sinned against the *Holy Spirit*, He *left* them.

By the time of Christ, in the Jews' second temple at Jerusalem—the temple restored by Herod—all the real elements of its former glory had ceased to exist. Priests were no longer admitted into ministry by Levitical descent and by the sacred anointing; instead, they were formally appointed. Even the office of high priest could be attained through political conspiracy, crime or bribery. The priesthood had become corrupt. Even the rabbis admitted that the spirit of prophecy had departed.

Unfortunately, Israel's spiritual decay had penetrated even deeper. The priests could no longer be anointed with the holy oil because its very composition had been forgotten. And the sacred fire that had descended from heaven upon the altar of burnt offering that was to burn continually had long since become extinct.

Sadder still, the holy of holies stood empty. The golden ark of the covenant and its mercy seat of solid gold had been missing since the Babylonian captivity. Absent also were the priceless articles the ark had contained: the two tablets of the law; a pot of manna preserved from the desert; Aaron's rod that budded as a symbol of his divine, authoritative priesthood. But the greatest tragedy of all was the absence of the *shechinah* cloud of glory that had once dwelt in the holy of holies.

Throughout Israel's forty wilderness years the glistening cloud had hovered above the ark of the covenant whenever the tribes were encamped; when they were on the move, it expanded to a pillar of cloud that guided them by day and a pillar of fire that guided and guarded them by night. Now the holy of holies stood dark and empty except for a large stone occupying the place where the ark with the mercy seat had once stood. Upon this stone the high priest sprinkled the blood on the day of atonement.

The mercy seat, which in Hebrew means "bloody covering," no longer covered Israel's sins. For centuries this blood-spattered lid of pure gold had hidden the record of Israel's iniquities and transgressions. But now no cleansed, anointed high priest stood before that mercy seat and cried from a compassionate heart for God's pardon and forgiveness. Instead, the broken law cried out, witnessing against Israel and appealing to God for judgment.

It was into this dreadful state of spiritual decline that Jesus appeared. Haggai had prophesied that the Lord would fill this temple with His glory (Hag. 2:7), but when Jesus came preaching the kingdom of God, healing the sick, forgiving sins and casting out demons, the chief priests and scribes were blind to the ways and works of the very God they purported to serve.

Accustomed to the spiritual decay, Israel's spiritual leaders

---

*The greatest tragedy of all
was the absence of the
shechinah cloud of glory that had
once dwelt in the holy of holies.*

---

preferred their man-made traditions rather than the truth. Quoting Isaiah the prophet, Jesus rebuked them because they valued the letter of the law more than the power of God:

> He answered and said to them, "Well did Isaiah prophesy of you hypocrites, as it is written:
> 'This people honors Me with their lips,
> But their heart is far from me.
> And in vain they worship Me,
> Teaching as doctrines the commandments of men.'
> For laying aside the commandment of God, you hold the tradition of men—the washing of pitchers and cups, and many other such things you do." And He said to them, "All too well you reject the commandment of God, that you may keep your tradition" (Mark 7:6-9).

But not all eyes were blind to Christ's majesty. John, a former fisherman and a faithful disciple, declared:

> And the Word became flesh and dwelt among us, and we beheld His glory, the glory as of the only begotten of the Father, full of grace and truth (John 1:14).

At the close of the first day of the Jewish Feast of Tabernacles,

119

for example, the priests and the people observed a ceremony involving the illumination of the temple. In the court of the women, great, golden lampstands were set up, their lamps furnished with wicks made from the old, worn breeches and girdles of the priests. Then the lamps were filled with oil and lighted.

As men, singing hymns and songs of praise, danced with flaming torches in their hands, the magnificent temple blazed with light. That man-made light, shining out of the temple and penetrating the night, served as a nostalgic reminder of the *shechinah* that had once filled the temple.

It is no coincidence that only a few days later Jesus stood in the temple court and boldly proclaimed to the crowd thronging about Him: "*I* am the light of the world. He who follows Me shall not walk in the darkness, but have the light of life" (John 8:12). The light of God's glory had returned to the temple, fulfilling Haggai's prophecy.

On the last day of the Feast of Tabernacles Jesus stood in the temple court quietly watching as the priest, according to custom, returned from the Pool of Siloam. He was carrying a golden pitcher of water, which he poured out on the base of the altar.

The rabbis interpreted this ceremony as symbolic of the annual rainfall supposedly determined by God at that feast, but Jesus realized that it foreshadowed the joyous outpouring of the Holy Spirit predicted in Isaiah 12:3. Jesus, refusing to revere their dead rituals, stepped forward and cried in a loud voice:

If anyone thirsts, let him come to Me and drink. He who believes in Me, as the Scripture has said, out of his heart will flow rivers of living water (John 7:37-38).

---

*Thousands of believers, ministers and
congregations across our land are
awakening to the reality that the glory
has departed from many of our churches.*

John, the disciple who recorded these events, went on to explain that Jesus was speaking of the Spirit, whom believers would receive after Jesus was glorified and raised to honor (v. 39).

What to Do When the Glory Departs

Jesus wept bitterly as He prophesied the fate of Jerusalem and its magnificent temple. In rejecting Him, Israel had rejected the blood that atoned for sin and removed guilt. They had refused to recognize the blood that would ratify the new covenant. They had reviled the delivering, protecting blood of God's Passover Lamb. Having rejected God's merciful provision, Jerusalem and the Jewish religious system plunged toward judgment and destruction. The hour of Israel's visitation was at an end (Luke 19:42-44; 21:24).

Thousands of believers, ministers and congregations across our land are awakening to the reality that the glory has departed from many of our churches. How can judgment be turned and destruction be averted? How can we bring back the glory?

Four sure steps for averting judgment are outlined in the familiar words of 2 Chronicles 7:14 (KJV):

> If my people, which are called by my name, shall
> humble themselves, and pray and seek my face, and

turn from their wicked ways; then will I hear from heaven, and will forgive their sin, and will heal their land.

We Must Humble Ourselves

It's hard to humble yourself and confess that the glory has departed from your life, but that's the first step to restoration. We must deal with our own sin. How? It's very simple. Admit it and quit it! Ask for divine forgiveness, deliverance and restoration.

What do you do about the sins of others? Forgive them. Give up your right to hurt them because they hurt you. If you want to see the glory return, freely forgive the sins and failures of others and stop criticizing and holding grudges.

We Must Pray

If you've lost track of the glory, it's because you've lost track of prayer. Luke recorded in Acts 19 that everyone in Asia Minor had heard of Jesus because of the church at Ephesus. But forty years later John reported that this same church had lost its first love (Rev. 2). Prayer had become a mere ritual, not a heart-consuming, driving force. They no longer had a fervent love for Jesus.

If your love is lukewarm, if prayer is a duty or drudgery rather than a delight, there is a remedy. Ask the Holy Spirit to plant within you the desire and the discipline to pray. Set a time each day to minister as a praying priest before God in the sanctuary of your soul.

The glory departs when we constantly seek what God can do for us instead of worshipping Him because of who He is for us.

We Must Seek God's Face

Have you ever noticed that 2 Chronicles 7:14 doesn't say "seek God's *hand*"? No, it commands: "Seek His *face*." We are not to seek only God's hand—what He can do for us, what He can give us. The "me-ism" mentality has got to go. If we want to see the power of His hand, we must seek the approval of His face—His smile; His nod; His correcting, reassuring glance; His full attention. The glory departs when we constantly seek what God can *do* for us instead of worshipping Him because of who He *is* for us.

We Must Turn From Our Wicked Ways

Regardless of the personal cost or sacrifice, we must turn away from the things that are displeasing to the Holy Spirit. We must not allow the cares and pressures of this world to distract us.

You can listen to a thousand sermons a day and not be changed. But if you humble yourself and choose to spend an hour every day in the presence of God, ministering to Him as a praying priest and interceding for yourself and for others, something supernatural will happen. His glory will return and transform your life and your family.

Interceding at the Mercy Seat

God has called me to raise up 300,000 intercessors who will stand daily before Him, mourning and repenting for the sins of our land, claiming His covenant promises and crying out to Him for mercy.

Jeremiah, the weeping prophet, declared:

> Through the Lord's *mercies* we are not consumed,
> Because His compassions fail not.
> They are new every morning;
> Great is Your faithfulness (Lam. 3:22-23, italics mine).

God never runs out of mercy. His mercies are as good today as they were yesterday.

I think about my yesterdays, growing up in the home of an alcoholic. I recall the yesterdays I spent in a psychiatric ward. I remember how devastated I felt when it seemed my ministry was over after I left Beverly Hills Baptist Church. But when I answered God's call to become a praying priest, the Lord's mercy rewrote my life. God led me to Rockwall, Texas, to birth a mighty church and now to take His prayer message to our nation.

Do you know what that says to me? It says that if there is mercy for *one* man in America, *everyone* can receive that mercy. It's not too late for you or your family. It's not too late for your church. And it's not too late for our nation. Unlike Jerusalem, our hour of visitation is not over. We don't have much time left, but it's enough time to answer God's call and become praying priests.

A human being filled with the power and presence of the

> *If there is mercy for one man in*
> *America, everyone can receive that mercy.*
> *It's not too late for you or your family.*
> *It's not too late for your church.*

Holy Spirit is one of God's choicest gifts to His church. A 300,000-member army of praying priests, filled with the power and presence of the Holy Spirit, could be God's most gracious gift to a nation that has become corrupt and gives no thought to Him.

The Holy Spirit is sifting and testing believers. He is calling out His army right now. If you will shoulder your responsibilities and claim your sacred privileges, you can have a part in averting the judgments, recovering the anointing and bringing back the glory. You can be on the front lines of the prayer army that kicks in the gates of hell.

You are a priest. It's time to enter into your priesthood.

NOTES

Chapter 1

1. Alexander Roberts and James Donaldson, eds., *The Ante-Nicene Fathers*, vol. 1, *Against Heresies* (Grand Rapids: Eerdmans, 1973), p. 409.

Chapter 3

1. W.J. Hollenweger, *The Pentecostals: The Charismatic Movement in the Churches* (Minneapolis: Augsburg Publishing House, 1972), p. 112.